The Four Sax Virtuosos

Copyright © 2021 José Luis Hinojosa

All rights reserved.

ISBN-13: 979-8-46-528505-6

THE FOUR SAX VIRTUOSOS

Musical Wisdom from the Experts

By

JOSÉ LUIS HINOJOSA, MD, MHA

Illustrations (incl. Cover)
José Luis Hinojosa, MD, MHA

Contents –

Dedication	p 6
Acknowledgments	p 8
Introduction	p 13
Prologue	p 31
Chapter 1: Mother on a Mission	p 39
Chapter 2: The First Sax Virtuoso	p 47
Chapter 3: The Second Sax Virtuoso	p 67
Chapter 4: The Third Sax Virtuoso	p 103
Chapter 5: The Fourth Sax Virtuoso	p 133
Epilogue	p 171
Saxophonists Speak	p 177
About the Author	p 185

DEDICATION –

I DEDICATE THIS BOOK to anyone who is currently on the path to self-discovery, self-worth, and self-realization, either through music or another art.

I also dedicate this book to all my music colleagues. Without your music, life would... B♭. (Sorry, I couldn't help myself.)

In addition, I dedicate this book to the following saxophone mentors who go above and beyond the notes on the music score:
- Dr. Wally Wallace, of The Saxophone Academy.
- Johnny Ferreira, of HowToPlaySaxophone.org
- Nigel McGill, of McGill Music Sax School.
- Jay Metcalf, of Better Sax.
- Jamie Anderson, of Get Your Sax Together.

Thank you all for your invaluable teachings!

I also dedicate this book my lovely wife, Maria Elena, whose love and support have allowed me to grow and develop my love for music, and my repertoire. During my practices at home, she'll say things like, "Didn't you play that song... four times already?"

I additionally dedicate this book to my children, JL, Laura, and Alexis. I love you and I am forever proud of you.

Lastly, I dedicate this book to my grandchildren, Darely, Geri, Brianna, Eric, and Ari. Hopefully, one or five of you will find joy in music as I have. I love you!

ACKNOWLEDGMENTS –

I AM GRATEFUL TO all my music-loving friends, musicians and non-musicians alike. For it is this love, this appreciation of music that bonds us. And it doesn't matter what style or what type of music it is. What matters is that it touches us profoundly - in our hearts, in our souls. And we *feel* that touch because we are alive. In fact, many times we are alive *because of the music*. Music that transports us to another time, another place. A place we love to visit, even if only in our minds, in our memories, in our hearts, and especially deep in our souls.

I am grateful that there is an *acoustic hierarchy* in orchestras. That is to say, orchestral sounds typically go from soft to loud (or, in musical terms, from *piano* to *forte*) as follows: strings, woodwinds, and finally brasses. Why am I grateful for such a hierarchy? Because it led to...

Well, I'll let you go on to the next paragraph and find out for yourself.

I am grateful to Adolphe Sax, who had a dream - a dream of combining the best qualities of the orchestral instruments of his time. And in doing so, he... *created an instrument with the tonal qualities of the woodwinds, the projection of the brasses, and the flexibility of the strings.*[1] This champion of all instruments is universally known as the *saxophone, sax,* or *saxo*. The saxophone's beginnings (its genesis, if you will) took place in the 1840s and Sax patented his invention in 1846 Paris.[2]

FOOTNOTES

1. Segell, M. (2005), The Devil's Horn: The Story of the Saxophone, from Noisy Novelty to King of Cool, Picador, New York, p. 16.
2. https://www.yamaha.com/en/musical_instrument_guide/saxophone/structure/

MY NOTES

THE FOUR SAX VIRTUOSOS

INTRODUCTION –

Music doesn't lie. If there is something to be changed in this world, then it can only happen through music.
~ Jimi Hendrix[3]

IN THIS DAY AND AGE OF SOCIETAL, interpersonal, and political unrest there is one prevailing theme: *systemic disrespect*. It is blatantly obvious that people no longer respect each other, no longer care for authority, no longer appreciate our military's service, no longer value their country nor their flag. Everyone is disrespecting everyone. Common courtesies are obsolete, and the ensuing anger only fuels more contempt. Confrontations are seen everywhere – in person, via the internet, and in the media – and in all walks of life. Verbal and physical clashes are spreading like the wildfires of California. Our country is on the verge of chaos and anarchy... and something must be done now to prevent this impending self-destruction.

How can we minimize racial and gender inequalities? How can we curtail the ever-growing lack of respect? How can common decencies be reintroduced into our lives, our communities, our country? I believe the answer is simple, but it must first start at the home.

To make meaningful and impactful change, our children (starting at an early age) must be taught right from wrong. Of course, this must first begin at the home; then it must be reinforced at school; and finally, righteousness must be encouraged everywhere else outside of the home or the school. Indeed, systemic disrespect will require systemic change.

It would be easy to say, "That's impossible!" No, it is not impossible – it may take lots of effort from lots of people, but it's not impossible. It is in fact, very possible... and quite simple. All we have to do is *lead by example*.

We humans have a knack for learning from others' behaviors and actions, from seeing what they *do* rather than learning from what they *say*. Their words and speeches lose their impact, their *umph*, by the time they reach our ears.

Enter... the musical arts.

What does all this have to do with music? Simple – great music educators are in a unique position to lead by example, to inspire their students to grow and develop as productive members of society, to learn and follow the Golden Rule of treating others' as they'd like to be treated. In fact, great instructors inspire their students to become better versions of themselves. And in so doing, these students give of themselves more readily, they compose new music, and through their music they provide joy and happiness to the masses. In other words, great musicians are in the business of healing, of serving, of creating magic, of allowing us to find... love. Yes, love.

I've always believed that great music is just like a recipe for a great meal - to make it succulent, to make it memorable, to make it wonderful, the first ingredient is always love. And it's not just the first ingredient, it's also the *magic* ingredient!

- • -

Indeed, those are big words: healing, service, magic and love. Music is that, and so much more. According to Max Lerman, Hospice and Palliative Care Music Therapist, here are some of the benefits of music on health and well-being[4]:

1. ***It's good for your Heart.*** Music can lower your blood pressure, it can reduce your heart rate, and it, and decrease *cortisol* (the stress hormone) levels. In the operating room, where patients' stress levels can be quite high, music can oftentimes relieve the anxiety.

   At the end of this chapter, I've listed a number of clinical trials that examined the effects of music intervention on procedural anxiety.[5-14] These studies differ in the types of procedures performed (e.g., colonoscopy versus cystoscopy - in the former, a tube is introduced into the colon; in the latter, a tube is introduced into the urinary bladder). The studies also differ in the types of music played, whether the music was chosen by the patient versus nature sounds, and in the length of the procedure and its timing (that is, was the music played before or after the procedure).

   Early in my medical career, I frequently assisted a surgeon who performed the entire surgery while expertly whistling relaxing tunes. It was always magical!

2. ***It elevates your Mood.*** Music can increase *serotonin* and *endorphin* levels - the former is the "mood stabilizer" hormone; the latter is the "feel good" hormone. In addition, music can boost dopamine production in the brain, which helps relieve anxiety and depression. Music is also processed in the *amygdala*, near the base of the brain. The amygdala is where emotions are given meaning, remembered, and attached to certain things (that is, *emotional memories* are formed in the amygdala). That's why a particular song can magically transport a person to another time, another place. We attach fond memories to certain songs.

Recently, I was playing solo saxophone (with backing tracks) at a health food restaurant. And just as a stressed-out nurse walked in the door, I started to play Roberta Flack's hit song "Killing Me Softly." Her entire complexion changed! She said aloud, "Hey, that's my favorite song!" and proceeded to start filming with her cellular phone. She was smiling and moving to the music the whole time - and I thought her scrubs even appeared a bit brighter than when she first walked in!

In 2003, I won my very first martial arts World Championship in Cancún, Mexico. That night, during a celebration fiesta, one particular song was played several times by the DJ - it was *the* song of the moment and it was also the first time I'd ever heard it. It was a salsa song by the Queen of Salsa, Celia Cruz, entitled "La Vida es un Carnaval" (*Life is a Carnival*). Nowadays, every time I hear that song, I'm instantly transported to that championship experience! What an uplifting feeling!

3. ***It can help Dementia patients.*** Although there is no cure for senile dementia or Alzheimer's Disease, music therapy has been shown to relieve some of its symptoms.[15-18] Music therapy can calm an agitated patient and decrease aggressive behaviors.

A few years ago, I was treating an elderly couple, both in their 80s. The husband was afflicted with heart problems and the wife suffered several severe comorbid conditions, including advanced dementia.

One day, during a routine follow-up on her dementia, we weren't getting anywhere. It was one of her bad days. The patient was staring blankly at nothing in particular and the husband was supportive, ever by her side.

Then it occurred to me.

I asked the husband, "Is it okay if I show you a little video on my phone? It's only 2 minutes." He asked what it was about and I said that I had started playing the saxophone again (after a 42-year hiatus), and I had recorded myself on my phone, just to see how it sounded. The husband smiled and said, "Sure!" So I took out my phone and pushed play on my practice version of Frank Sinatra's "Fly Me to the Moon."

What happened next is one of the reasons I became a doctor... and a musician.

The patient's eyes suddenly lit up. Her face came alive... and she started singing along with the video! Even her foot started tapping!
At that moment, my heart was full. And my eyes watered ever so slightly.

Here was a woman who didn't recognize her husband of 60 years, who didn't know what day it was, who didn't remember if she ate or if she didn't, who was totally dependent on others for her personal care. Yet, she *knew* every... single... word to this song!

When the video finished, the husband said, "Doctor Hinojosa, my wife used to be a pretty good singer."

"I believe you," I said. "She still has a nice vibrato!" Then I said to her, "You're a good singer, Mrs. Ross." Mrs. Ross smiled... and slowly, her eyes left us again.

This encounter confirmed to me that music is powerful. Music can bring back someone who is lost. Music is powerful *and* music heals. Indeed, music is a powerful healer. And so what if it heals only momentarily? It heals!

4. **It eases Pain.** Music therapy can assist in pain management by reducing stress levels and providing strong competing stimuli to the pain signals that reach the brain. Music has been shown to significantly reduce the perceived pain intensity, especially in the elderly, in the intensive care unit, and in palliative care.[19-20]

5. **It can help Cancer patients.** Music therapy is one of the relaxation techniques that have been shown to

reduce some of the chemotherapy side effects (such as nausea, vomiting, pain, and fatigue) and improve mood, sleep, physical function, and quality of life in cancer patients.[21]

6. ***It can help you Eat Less.*** Soft music is a major component of setting the right mood for weight management. Background soft music and dimmed lights during a meal can help people slow down while eating. Ultimately, this can result in less food consumption during one sitting.

7. ***It can increase your workout Endurance.*** Listening to upbeat workout music can boost physical performance and increase endurance during an intense exercise session.

In my tell-all autobiography, *Fighting to Heal*, I talk about the time I trained with Dan Inosanto (Bruce Lee's best friend) at the Aspen Academy of Martial Arts. Here's what I said about that special time in my life:[22]

Dan Inosanto provided all the equipment we needed for class. Jump ropes, 28-inch fighting sticks, 6-foot staffs, focus gloves, metal swords, and metal knives were in abundance. Every day, Dan would take out his cassette player and we'd jump rope to the 1976 Vicki Sue Robinson hit, Turn the Beat Around, *for two minutes at the beginning of class. Not only did the lively music get our circulation going, it also put us in the right mood off the bat - plus, it gave me some valuable footwork training.*

Next, we would perform stretching and warm-up exercises to the beat of Dan's drum, which he played with a stick. Every time we started a different exercise, he'd change the rhythm on the drum. That drum was loud, but not overpowering. It allowed us to feel what we were doing, to "get into it," to truly enjoy the moment.

The music and drum rhythms were of paramount importance that summer. They permitted us to grow as martial artists. Being a musician, I understood this right away - many students didn't, until Dan showed us.

One day, towards the end of the month, Dan had us jump rope without our usual music. The two minutes went on forever. It was odd listening to moans, groans, puffs, and irregular rhythms of ropes hitting the mat at different times. There certainly was no percussion rhythm one could follow, as when we "turned the beat around" to the music. Most of us tired easily without the energetic music's help.

- • -

So, how do you choose the right music school? Most people, especially the uninitiated, don't have the slightest idea. Yes, it can be a nightmare. So, to simplify the process, I believe you must first select the right *music teacher*.

With this in mind, I am basing the following recommendations on my innovative book, *TaeKwonDo for Everyone*, which delineates a few attributes of a good teacher.[23]

First and foremost, you must select a TEACHER. This is probably one of the most important decisions you will have to make, and it will certainly pave your way to a brighter and happier music future if you select the right teacher for you and your family. A qualified musician or a music educator who has your success and personal advancement at heart will certainly help you achieve more than you ever could on your own. The following are a few reliable marks of a good teacher:

- **Respect** – A good teacher will receive and also give respect to students. While he/she may have set high standards for all students and appear at times demanding, he/she will not be demeaning.

- **Transparency** – The good teacher will have nothing to do with special musical licks or esoteric knowledge that will be available to only a select few students who may be deemed "worthy" at a later time. The school curriculum is written down and made available to students from legitimate schools. That way, students know what to expect and the curriculum can be scrutinized by students and parents alike.

- **Qualifications** – Anyone can buy a fake diploma online, but what about the teacher's true qualifications? Do a background check and identify if the teacher truly graduated from the conservatory he/she claims.

Besides the attributes of respect, transparency and qualifications, here are a few more things to consider when seeking the right music teacher for you and your family:[24-25]

a) **Word of Mouth.** Ask around for recommendations, especially look for teachers with successful track records of teaching your peers (if you're the one wanting to learn music). If the lessons are for your child, find out who's done well with your child's peers.

b) **Music Organizations.** Don't overlook local branches of national teachers' associations, such as Music Teachers National Association and the National Association for Music Education. These organizations can help you locate a qualified music instructor in your area. Also, don't forget music organizations at the state and local levels.

c) **Student Recitals.** If possible, attend a prospective teacher's student recital. Such an event can give you a general sense of the music school's culture and what type of music and/or instruments are strengths (or weaknesses). You'll also see first-hand how the music teacher acts in public and how he/she treats the disciples. Plus, you'll find out what age groups the instructor most commonly works with. You might even ponder if you see yourself (or your child) participating at next year's recital.

d) **Free Lessons.** Take advantage of a free, trial lesson, if available. If not available, ask if you can have one free lesson as a win-win scenario. You can explain the win-win as follows: It's a great opportunity for the teacher to find out if he/she is willing to take you on as a student, and you (as the prospective student) can also find out if you're willing to hire him/her as a music teacher.

e) **Questions?** Finally, ask lots of questions. Here are a few you may want to consider:
- What's the teacher's background as a teacher?
- What's the teacher's background as a musician?
- How much practice time (outside of the music school) is expected?
- What kinds of performance opportunities will be provided?
- What kinds of competitive opportunities will be provided?
- Is there any travel expected? If so, how often and to what locations?
- Will the students be able to video tape their lessons?
- Are Skype lessons or Zoom lessons available? If so, how often?
- How much music theory is involved?
- How much composition is involved?
- What are the weekly, monthly, and yearly expectations for students? For parents?

It may take several attempts for you to find the right teacher... and the right school. Go elsewhere if you feel your teacher is holding you back or not allowing you to participate in events that you feel may increase your musical knowledge.

- • -

As described above, the right music school – and one that fosters good moral values – can positively influence its students. Integrating the world of music into one's daily life, I believe, can lead to health, happiness, and harmony for the individual. In turn, this can help build freedom, justice, and peace in our society... especially in the face of a worldwide pandemic. After all, our society is made up of many individuals very much like you and me. And the cumulative effects of what is carried out by many is really what defines society's dynamics.

The more individuals in harmony, the more individuals playing music, the more individuals listening to and dancing to music, the more individuals reminiscing about happier days because of a song they've just heard, the more individuals finding joy and love... the less people will fight each other, and the increased likelihood that positive societal changes will ensue.

FOOTNOTES

3. https://www.brainyquote.com/quotes/jimi_hendrix_1 95416?src=t_music

4. https://www.northshore.org/healthy-you/9-health-benefits-of-music/

5. El-Hassan H, McKeown K, Muller AF. Clinical trial: music reduces anxiety levels in patients attending for endoscopy. Aliment Pharmacol Ther 2009; 30:718.

6. Hayes A, Buffum M, Lanier E, et al. A music intervention to reduce anxiety prior to gastrointestinal procedures. Gastroenterol Nurs 2003; 26:145.

7. López-Cepero Andrada JM, Amaya Vidal A, Castro Aguilar-Tablada T, et al. Anxiety during the performance of colonoscopies: modification using music therapy. Eur J Gastroenterol Hepatol 2004; 16:1381.

8. Chan YM, Lee PW, Ng TY, et al. The use of music to reduce anxiety for patients undergoing colposcopy: a randomized trial. Gynecol Oncol 2003; 91:213.

9. Yeo JK, Cho DY, Oh MM, et al. Listening to music during cystoscopy decreases anxiety, pain, and dissatisfaction in patients: a pilot randomized controlled trial. J Endourol 2013; 27:459.

10. Zengin S, Kabul S, Al B, et al. Effects of music therapy on pain and anxiety in patients undergoing port catheter placement procedure. Complement Ther Med 2013; 21:689.

11. Ni CH, Tsai WH, Lee LM, et al. Minimising preoperative anxiety with music for day surgery patients - a randomised clinical trial. J Clin Nurs 2012; 21:620.

12. Zhang ZS, Wang XL, Xu CL, et al. Music reduces panic: an initial study of listening to preferred music improves male patient discomfort and anxiety during flexible cystoscopy. J Endourol 2014; 28:739.

13. Angioli R, De Cicco Nardone C, Plotti F, et al. Use of music to reduce anxiety during office hysteroscopy: prospective randomized trial. J Minim Invasive Gynecol 2014; 21:454.

14. Uğraş GA, Yıldırım G, Yüksel S, et al. The effect of different types of music on patients' preoperative anxiety: A randomized controlled trial. Complement Ther Clin Pract 2018; 31:158.

15. Clark ME, Lipe AW, Bilbrey M. Use of music to decrease aggressive behaviors in people with dementia. J Gerontol Nurs 1998; 24:10.

16. Gerdner LA. Effects of individualized versus classical "relaxation" music on the frequency of agitation in elderly persons with Alzheimer's disease and related disorders. Int Psychogeriatr 2000; 12:49.

17. Cohen-Mansfield J. Nonpharmacologic interventions for inappropriate behaviors in dementia: a review, summary, and critique. Am J Geriatr Psychiatry 2001; 9:361.

18. van der Steen JT, van Soest-Poortvliet MC, van der Wouden JC, et al. Music-based therapeutic

interventions for people with dementia. Cochrane Database Syst Rev 2017; 5:CD003477.

19. Bradt J, Dileo C. Music interventions for mechanically ventilated patients. Cochrane Database Syst Rev 2014; :CD006902.

20. Ziehm S, Rosendahl J, Barth J, et al. Psychological interventions for acute pain after open heart surgery. Cochrane Database Syst Rev 2017; 7:CD009984.

21. Bradt J, Dileo C, Grocke D, Magill L. Music interventions for improving psychological and physical outcomes in cancer patients. Cochrane Database Syst Rev 2011;:CD006911.

22. *Fighting to Heal,* p 257-258.

23. *TaeKwonDo for Everyone,* p 183-184.

24. https://www.npr.org/sections/deceptivecadence/2012/06/18/155282661/finding-the-right-teacher-for-your-music-loving-kid

25. https://www.connollymusic.com/stringovation/finding-right-music-teacher

MY NOTES

MY NOTES

THE FOUR SAX VIRTUOSOS

Prologue –

> *A conductor should guide*
> *rather than command.*
> ~ Riccardo Muti[26]

- • -

IN JANUARY 2016, I WAS CHIEF OF STAFF at a hospital in rural Kansas when I attended a continuing medical education (CME) conference entitled *Chief of Staff Bootcamp*. The conference was hosted by The Institute for Medical Leadership® and it was designed for healthcare leaders.

At one point, the nearly one-hundred attendees took a self-assessment personality test to determine what color category we would be placed in – red, yellow, blue, or green. We were then divided into four groups, each group representing one of the aforementioned colors, of about 20-25 participants per group. For the ensuing exercise, each group was asked to select a leader, a representative, who would not only guide the group's problem-solving discussion, but would also have to present the group's conclusions and recommendations to the entire congregation.

THE FOUR SAX VIRTUOSOS

Our group huddled up in a circle and everyone was talking without rhyme or reason. Quickly realizing that this approach would get us nowhere, I said in a confident tone, "Okay, how are we going to do this?" As if this was the cue everyone had been secretly hoping for, the group instantly shushed and someone looked right at me and said, "I move that you represent the group." Before I could object – not that I was going to, mind you – someone else said, "I second the motion." And just like that, I became the group's leader, a sort of leader of leaders. I was in my element, and I loved it!

Susan Reynolds, MD, PhD, was the moderator for that particular exercise. She's also the author of the book, *Prescription for Lasting Success*. Here's what her book says about this type of interactive activity:[27]

> *I have found in my consulting work that balancing personality types in any given workgroup or team is a key ingredient for success. I have used the PACE™ Color Palette, a screening tool that uses four colors to determine basic personality traits, at several of my leadership workshops. It is basically a quick, simplified version of the well-known Myers-Briggs personality test.*
>
> *The test defines **red** personalities as those who are action-oriented, energetic, spontaneous, and fun, but who might work too quickly and get sloppy. They tend to have lower attention to detail.*
>
> ***Yellow** personalities are very process-oriented, focus on details, and may drive reds crazy with all their planning, agendas, policies, and procedures. Yellows also run the risk of getting stuck or bogged down with their processes.*

Blue *personalities are nice people who like to build consensus and make everyone happy. They are good listeners and are easy to get along with. But since they hate conflict so much, they tend to be slow to make decisions, because it takes time to get consensus from everyone without hurting anyone's feelings.*

Green *personalities are creative, out-of-the-box thinkers who are focused on strategy but who tend to work alone.*

Ideally, every workgroup should have a balance of all four personality types. This allows creative ideas to surface (green), a drive towards action to take place (red), a process for execution to be established (yellow), and a consensus that is easy to build (blue). By providing this balance, you maximize the group's success. But if just one component is missing, you risk having a lack of creative ideas (no green), reduced forward action (no red), less attention to details or order (no yellow), or weak camaraderie or agreement (no blue).

– • –

And so, I headed the Green Group with pride and efficiency. We arrived at viable solutions to the list of problems given to us. Next, it was time to report on each group's findings and recommendations.

The group leaders stood in the middle of the assembly hall, ready to address the rest of the conference participants. We were lined up in order: red, yellow, blue, and finally, green.

Each of the first three representatives spoke, followed by anemic applause. To me, none of the group leaders had displayed that wow factor needed to hook the audience, to capture their attention, to engage them in something of value. I saw this as a perfect opportunity to break the monotone pattern that had been established by the previous presenters.

I started off by saying, "Well, we've obviously saved the best for last!" To my surprise, the audience was suddenly anemic no more – they applauded with enthusiasm, eager to engage in what I was about to say. I continued, "As you know, green is the representative color of medicine, our noble profession. It is also the color that signifies life and growth. Thus, let me share with you how our group gave life to the following solutions we've agreed upon..."

I proceeded to delineate our group's assessments and recommendations. To say that we finished off with a bang would be an understatement. After the applause settled, I asked someone to take our picture. To me, that interactive session was the highlight of the entire trip.

- • -

So, what does this medical leadership conference have to do with this book? Plenty. *The Four Sax Virtuosos* is the story of four musicians/music educators, each with a particular set of values, personality traits, and attributes that make up the leaders, the role models, the music teachers depicted in the pages that follow.

Here's my full disclosure: Throughout this book, I use the PACE™ Palette (the one that was given to each of the attendees at the aforementioned *Chief of Staff Bootcamp*) in order to give a complete picture of each of the personality types described herein.

However, I believe that not everyone will be a perfect match regarding fitting into one of the four personality "colors." They simply won't be able to check all the boxes. Instead, most people tend to possess a few attributes from each of the categories, making them unique and special individuals.

Nonetheless, for the purposes of this book, the four protagonists will display typical attributes and characteristics of their assigned color.

Music students, both current and prospective, will better understand why their instructors say what they say and do what they do... for the most part. And after not only reading (but also studying) this book, you will have gained valuable insight that can help you select the right music teacher for you and your family. This, in turn, can serve as an integral step in the arduous road of improving our society's woes.

Good luck with your quest for personal improvement and self-enlightenment while positively impacting our society.

As always, please feel free to contact me if you have any comments, questions, or if you simply want to connect.

And let the music play on...
José Luis Hinojosa, MD, MHA

You can e-mail me at: **sales@BooksByDrHinojosa.com**

FOOTNOTES

26. https://www.slideshare.net/MusicandLeadership/7-music-leadership-quotes-to-inspire-you

27. Reynolds, S.F., MD, PhD, *Prescription for Lasting Success: Leadership Strategies to Diagnose Problems and Transform your Organization,* ©2012, John Wiley & Sons, Inc, Hoboken, NJ, p 132-133.

MY NOTES

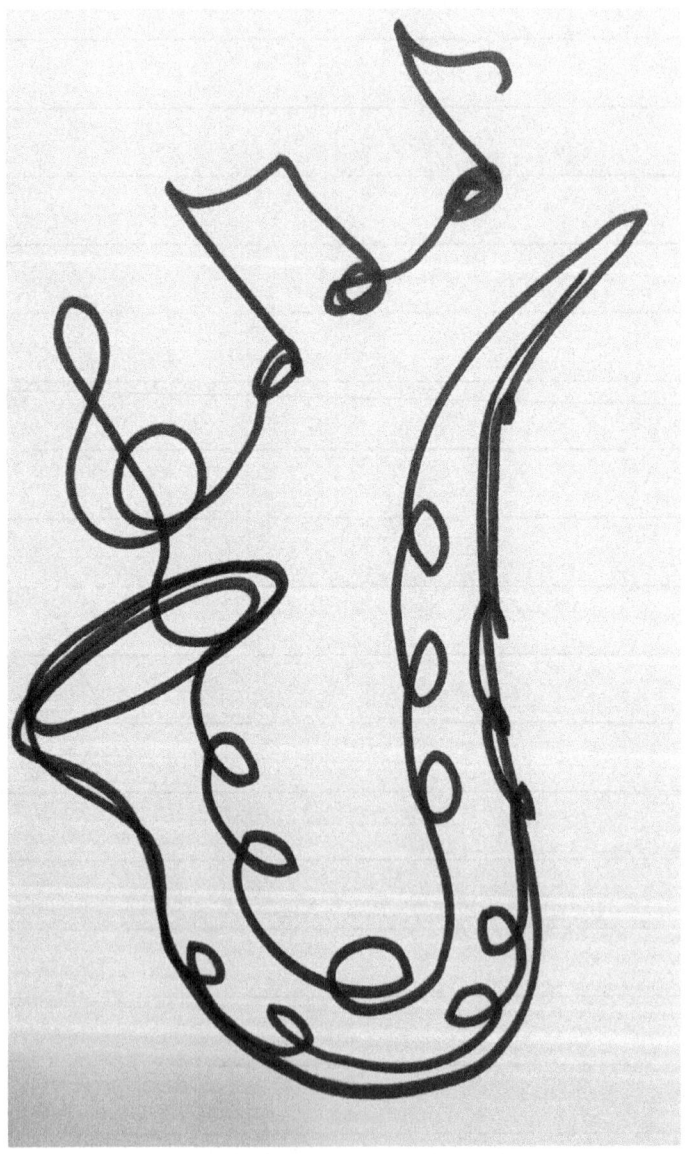

Chapter 1

MOTHER ON A MISSION

> *There is music in every child.*
> *The teacher's job is to find it*
> *and nurture it.*
> *~ Frances Clark*[28]

- • -

"C'MON IGGIE, WE'RE LATE!" said an exasperated Beverly Song.

"It's Ignatius, not Iggie." He said it again, only louder, "Ignatius!"

The Songs were new to town and Iggie had had a rough first day at school, so he snapped at his mother. He felt justified. Besides, it's never cool being the new kid in class. He hated the fact that only two weeks ago, he had left all his friends behind. No, he hadn't *left* them – he had *abandoned* them. Yeah, that's it. "Abandoned" is a stronger word, a stronger emotion, and

Iggie felt strongly about his family's recent move.

Beverly, a multi-tasking woman who would put Soccer Moms to shame, said without skipping a beat, "Well... whatever." And then she mumbled, "You'll always be Iggie to me."

"What? What did you say?"

"Nothing... nothing. C'mon, let's go."

Iggie dragged his feet, slumped his shoulders, and looked at the ground as he followed his mother into the car, a brand new, latest-model, German-engineered Mercedes Benz sedan with all the bells and whistles. The Songs would have nothing less.

Iggie sat in the back seat alone, leaving the front passenger seat vacant on purpose. Beverly thought about saying something but bit her tongue. They drove away as sad, angry Iggie stared into nothingness.

- • -

During the twenty-minute drive, Iggie didn't utter a word, although his mother tried several times to initiate a conversation. He just sat there, feeling sorry for himself. A plethora of questions flooded his brain. *Why does she still call me that? I hate it! Does she even care what I think?*

Let's face it, he wasn't a child anymore. Heck, he was 12 and he'd be a great musician one day. At least, that was his mother's plan anyway.

Iggie had several musical instruments at his disposal, none of which he enjoyed. He had been taking piano, voice and violin lessons since age 3 but nothing quite resonated with him.

That's when his zealous mother resorted to the *shotgun* approach and began purchasing an overabundance of instruments. She barraged him with so many that, according to her, "Something's gotta stick!"

Poor Iggie had to surf the web with caution. Whichever musical instrument happened to pop up on his laptop when Beverly hovered would surely arrive via Amazon the next day. Ergo, it is no surprise that Iggie owned a banjo, an accordion, a zither, and even a cowbell!

Iggie had participated in every musical production at JFK Elementary in Anytown, USA since the 1st grade. In his first stage appearance he was a rock. Anytown is the town where all his friends are probably playing and having fun this very instant.

Now, as a pre-teen, he was a musical prodigy. Well, at least to Beverly Song. One would think that Ignatius "Iggie" Song was rocking it, but one would be wrong. You see, Iggie abhorred music or anything having to do with music. He absolutely detested it. It was not for him; it was for her! His mother.

*She's the one who pushes and pushes, the one who wants to live her life through me... her only child,*Iggie pondered. *If she loves it so much, why doesn't she sign-up herself? There's old people in music.*

A lot of *why me's?* crisscrossed in his mind before Iggie was startled back into reality by a knock on the car door. It was his mother. She was standing outside and had been banging on that door for a while now.

As Iggie popped the door open, she rolled her eyes to the heavens and mouthed, "Finally!"

They had reached their destination – a prospective music education school in Newtown, USA. Iggie got out, half-heartedly pulling his attaché case behind him. His mother had stuffed a bunch of music scores in it. Who knows what was in there, but it sure was heavy. As he shuffled his feet, Iggie only looked at the ground.

"Look where you're going!" demanded his mother. Then, a recurring, unwanted visitor (a thought) appeared in her mind. It said, *The worst thing in the world is wasted talent.*

Iggie finally looked up and the first thing he saw was the corner street sign – it read *Main St.*

"Here we are," she proudly announced. "I found out that Main Street is where all the music schools are in this municipality!"

Beverly Song was on a mission – a mission to find a music school for her only child. But not any school would do. *No Sir'ee Bob!* Her precious Iggie needed to be in the best!

How would she find the best?

Easy.

She would interview the prospective instructors. No, not *interview*, that's too "nice" of a word... she would *drill* the prospects. Yes, that's what she was going to do. She would drill and drill until she got what she wanted, until she hit the jackpot, until she struck gold. Personally, Beverly favored diamonds, but she didn't mind a gold bar or two... as long as she accomplished her goal of finding the best for Iggie.

As a Music Mom, Beverly was second to none. She was fanatical about it. Rumor had it that she once dressed up as Annie when she attended one of Iggie's school musicals. Yes, she sported a red wig and overdid the freckles on her cheeks - she looked like she was going to war! Sadly, Iggie didn't have a speaking (or singing) role. That time, he was a tree. Nonetheless, Beverly went all out. Perhaps this Annie anecdote was true, perhaps it was only hearsay.

But whether or not she had resorted to *war paint* is irrelevant, so she'd said in her defense. "Irrelevant" because Beverly was always prepared. She never left anything to chance. And one way she prepared was by writing everything down – all her notes, thoughts, questions, and *what if* scenarios. She remembered her physician father telling her many years earlier: "If it isn't written down, it never happened!"

So, Beverly wrote everything down and she was prepared. She knew exactly what questions to ask. More specifically, she knew what questions she needed *answered*. Never mind what Iggie wanted or didn't want.

This was her show.

She could hear the Announcer on the overhead speakers: "And now... The Beverly Song Show!"
It sure has a nice ring to it, she thought with a smile.
Beverly Song would not be denied. Newtown, USA and Main Street would soon find out that she was a mother on a mission.

THE FOUR SAX VIRTUOSOS

Oh, what a mother!

And oh, what a mission!

FOOTNOTES

28. https://www.pinterest.co.uk/pin/224968943860946135/

THE FOUR SAX VIRTUOSOS

Chapter 2

THE FIRST SAX VIRTUOSO

Music should always be an adventure.
~ Coleman Hawkins[29]

- • -

AS BEVERLY OPENED THE FRONT DOOR of the music education establishment, she couldn't help but notice the red saxophone on the wall. There was something about that saxo... It was as if a powerful improvised solo emanated from it and struck her, punching her deeply in her soul. Well, first in her gut, then her soul. She suddenly felt an overwhelming sense of *adventure*. All the while, a soft jazz backing track played in the background. Beverly was momentarily mesmerized.

"Mom, what are you doing?"

The music suddenly stopped. Beverly shook her head and said, "Huh? What?" She saw Iggie's concerned look and managed to say, "Oh, it's nothing. C'mon, let's find out who runs this operation."

- • -

"Hi there!" shouted someone from a nearby practice room. Beverly saw a short, stocky man waving at them, so she awkwardly waved back.

The man who waved looked like he was the one in charge. He was leading his solo saxophone student in an exercise that looked like a lot of fun. The energy in the air was palpable. There were crescendos and short, sharply separated staccato notes every few seconds. After the etude was completed, the man assigned one of his assistants to take over.

The man exited the practice room and slammed the door behind him, not realizing his strength. Easily, that would have measured a 7.0 on the Richter scale. Even inattentive Iggie noticed this. He had been taught to always gently close the door when exiting a room, but maybe he'd been doing it wrong all along. Maybe this fun-loving instructor had a different philosophy.

"Howdy folks! I'm Saxophone Virtuoso Red... as in the color of *fire*! Get it?"

Beverly and Iggie were overwhelmed by this man's exuberance that all they could do was... nothing. They were unexpectedly frozen in place.

The music educator wasn't about to let his guests' paralysis dampen his mood, so he continued, "Welcome to Red Saxophone Music Academy!" He extended his right hand to Beverly, she instinctively reciprocated and was quickly and efficiently shaken vigorously. Her entire body continued to reverberate for a second or two after he let go of her hand. (The ole *reverb* effect in music.)

Seeing this burst of uncontrollable energy from the music educator, Iggie prayed he would be spared from such... excitement. Too late – before he knew it, the man grabbed him by the arm and shook him with a gusto Iggie had never experienced before. After finally being released from what he thought was a death grip, Iggie noticed a strange sensation, one that he'd never felt before. It was a throbbing, crescendo-like pain that enveloped his entire head. It was the worst headache he'd ever experienced. He felt like throwing up.

After the initial *pleasantries*, the music educator led them to his office and said, "Sit yourselves down, won't you?"

As the sax virtuoso closed the door behind them, this time at a more reasonable 4.0 on the Richter scale, Beverly noticed the man's fedora – it was red instead of the typical black she'd seen in other saxophonists. Besides, it was also quite ragged, which probably meant he'd worn it for a long time. But what struck her the most was not how *old* the fedora looked, but rather how *unkempt* it was. To Beverly, musical prodigy's mother extraordinaire, the fedora didn't appear to be properly fitted. Plus, the rim/visor angle was just too much for her taste.

That is so unacceptable, she thought. *It looks terrible!*

If there was one thing that truly irked Beverly, it was a person's sheer disregard to detail and orderliness, especially in something so important (she believed) as music education. Saxophone Virtuoso Red had certainly pushed her pet peeve buttons. He was obviously sloppy, perhaps even disrespectful -

THE FOUR SAX VIRTUOSOS

Iggie wasn't the only one who saw the door slamming. And the man apparently wasn't bothered by an improperly fitting fedora, nor by an untidy T-shirt.

SV Red
You like my T-shirt?
(*sticks out his chest*)

The man's T-shirt read: *I might look like I'm listening to you, but in my head I'm playing my saxophone.*

Iggie
Cool shirt!

Beverly was not impressed.

Although she had just met him, Saxophone Virtuoso Red had not made a good first impression. Beverly Song's test hadn't even started and this man was already flunking miserably.

She recalled a piece of advice she likes to give her son before each of his music lessons: *Remember, Iggie, always dress for success and you will shine like a star on stage. And why do I say this? Because looking good is the first step in being a good musician. I know, I know I've told you this a million times, but that's because I love you.*

- • -

As soon as Saxophone Virtuoso Red sat in his chair, he said, "So, are you both signing up for lessons?"
"Actually," said Beverly, "before we discuss any of that, I have some questions for you." She didn't wait for an acknowledgement or anything, she just pulled out her iPad

from her handbag and started clicking away at the screen.

"Sure…" said the music educator, hoping she'd get right to the point. It was hard for him to sit still for very long.

Beverly
First of all, Iggie, my son here…

Iggie
(*interrupting*)
Ignatius, mother, not Iggie.
(*to SV Red*)
Ignatius, sir.

SV Red
Ee-nation?

Iggie
Ig-na-tius…
(*trying to justify*)
You know, like the fiery one.
(*growls his face silently and raises a claw hand*)

SV Red
Fiery? Oh… fiery!

Beverly
(*raises her hands to stop everything*)
That's not important!
That's… *not* important.

After she was satisfied that she had regained control, she continued.

Beverly *(cont'd.)*
Just call him Song...
or Mr. Song.

SV Red
Mr. Song?

Beverly
Yes. Mister Song.
I'll have you know he's a musical prodigy,
and
he's gonna perform
in Carnegie Hall one day!

SV Red
Carnegie Hall? Really?

Beverly
Yes, really.

SV Red
That's wonderful!
Most of our students are musical
prodigies themselves!
(*turns to Iggie*)
You'll fit right in!

Beverly
Not so fast.
We still have to
go over a few things.

SV Red
Right, your questions...
(*he shifted in his seat*)

Beverly
Right. First off, why is your fedora red?

SV Red
In music, the color red exemplifies
passion and fervor. At Red Saxophone Music
Academy, we've found that passionate musicians
connect better with their audiences.

Beverly
I didn't know that.
I thought passion was for ballads
and red meant that
you should have some fire.
Be unstoppable.

SV Red
That too.
Our passionate students
are unstoppable.
(*he slid his hand along his fedora's brim*)

Beverly
Very well, then.
(*turns to her iPad*)
Ah, yes...
I don't want my son to be
just another number.
It's obvious that his youth
can inspire others and he can

Beverly *(cont'd.)*
do a lot for your academy.
But, what can *you* do for him?

SV Red
(without hesitation)
He can start out on one of our
Alto Mark VI as a loaner!
*(when Beverly didn't respond
with great excitement, he added)*
Those are the best saxophones
in the world.

Beverly
*(taps some keys on her iPad,
her mind somewhere else)*
That's good...

SV Red
Plus, he'd be joining the
best music academy in the country!

Beverly
Yes, I saw that on your sign.

SV Red
We're very proud of that!
Our students not only participate
in a lot of competitions, they win!

Beverly
Oh, they win, do they?

SV Red
Let me put it this way:
We don't eat competition
for breakfast... we *devour* it!

Beverly
I see...
(*quickly punches notes at her iPad*)
So, what kind of competitions?

SV Red
Mainly woodwind...
Jazz and Classical.
But we also excel on most
of the instruments typical
of philharmonic orchestras.

Beverly
I get the Classical.
But you also teach Jazz?

SV Red
Yes, that is correct.

Beverly
But isn't Jazz just a bunch
of wrong notes?

SV Red
(*laughs loudly*)
You're thinking Jazz *improvisation*.
And no, improvisation is not a bunch
of wrong notes. It's actually quite
complex... plus it's

> **SV Red** *(cont'd.)*
> tremendously exhilarating!
> *(he shakes as if a chill
> just went down his spine)*
>
> **Beverly**
> Okay... next question:
> What conservatory of music
> did you attend?
>
> **SV Red**
> *(proudly)*
> Musicians Institute in Los Angeles...
> It's the stuff of legends!
>
> **Beverly**
> What was that?
> Is that a *real* conservatory?
>
> **SV Red**
> *(impatiently takes out a flyer
> and points to something)*
> Here. Here's my alma mater.
> It's ranked #20 out of the top
> conservatories of music in the country.
> Got my p-h-d in music performance!

Beverly examined the flyer. It highlighted things such as "Amongst the Best in the Country" and Saxophone Virtuoso Red's degree, which was written as "PHD," all capitals. Beverly instantly noticed the typographical error – even she knew that a Doctor of Philosophy degree was referred to as "PhD," certainly not "PHD!" She also knew that PhD's in music are more for academic settings, whereas performance-oriented doctorates are typically DMA's, Doctor of Musical Arts. She made a notation on her iPad and went on with her due process.

Beverly
Moving right along...
Will my son be able to use the
instruments he already has?
I just bought him a very expensive
zither, direct lineage to the great
Johann Petzmayer, and I'd rather
not spend any more than I have to.

SV Red
No problem! At Red Saxophone Music
Academy, the saxophone is our #1
instrument. So, as I mentioned earlier...
(*but you were too busy to listen,* he thought)
We'll start out with one of our top-of-the-line
loaners. A Selmer Mark VI from Paris.

Beverly
Okay... (she was afraid to ask)
What color will it be?

SV Red, Beverly, and Iggie
(*simultaneously*)
Red!
(*they all laughed,
SV Red the loudest*)

SV Red
We encourage students' personalities
and individual sounds to outshine

SV Red *(cont'd.)*
others on stage. And we've found
that that happens more often
with our red saxophones.

Beverly
Good...
*(she made a notation and thought
'a man who thinks like I do')*
Last question:
Can you make sure there's no "heavy lifting"?
I don't want my son to get hurt.

SV Red
Well, that may be a problem.

Beverly
What do you mean?

SV Red
Here, we learn by doing, not
by sitting around reading fingering
charts or Circle of Fifths.

Beverly
I understand... but can you
guarantee me that my son
won't get hurt?

SV Red
At Red Saxophone Music Academy,
playing the saxophone *is* a contact sport!
And I can guarantee you the following:
Your son is certainly gonna feel...

SV Red *(cont'd.)*
*(he raises a hand and extends
a finger on each item)*
neck pain, thumb pain, and
pain on the kisser!
I can guarantee you that!
(laughs out loud)

Beverly
Okay, I guess we're done.
(gets her things and stands up)
We'll get back with you. Thank you.
(exits the office; Iggie follows)

SV Red
(waves after them)
Hope to see you soon,
Mr. Song!
(under his breath)
Poor kid. Looks like a song
that doesn't want to be sung.

- • -

The Personal and Company Effectiveness (PACE™) Palette gives the following attributes of *adventurous* personalities, such as Saxophone Virtuoso Red. Here then, are the negative characteristics (the stressors, irritators, and aggravators) followed by the positive characteristics of Reds:

Aggravators of REDS

- Reds can be impatient.

- Reds tend to be impulsive.

- Reds are not great listeners.

- Reds get bored easily and are restless.

- Reds don't like details.

- Reds hate being "fenced in" or cornered.

- Reds like to break rules, especially those that don't make sense.

Strengths of REDS

- Reds are competitive; they love a challenge.
- Reds enjoy freedom and flexibility.
- Reds are charismatic, charming, and love the spotlight.
- Reds are typically the life of the party.
- Reds are visionaries.
- Reds are bottom-line oriented.
- Reds like to do things their own way.
- Reds bounce back quickly - defeats are only temporary.

THE FOUR SAX VIRTUOSOS

– • –

Here are a few questions to consider regarding the encounter between Beverly, Iggie, and Saxophone Virtuoso Red:

1) Do any of these positive or negative characteristics of red personalities sound like Saxophone Virtuoso Red?

2) What did Beverly Song like about Saxophone Virtuoso Red and/or his academy?

3) What did Beverly Song dislike about Saxophone Virtuoso Red and/or his academy?

4) Is Beverly Song likely to enroll Iggie in this academy? Why or why not?

5) Should Saxophone Virtuoso Red accept Iggie as a student? Why or why not?

6) On a scale of 0 – 5, with 0 being the absolute worst and 5 being the absolute best, how would you rate Saxophone Virtuoso Red in regard to the three markers of a good teacher mentioned in the *Introduction*?

- Respect: 0   1   2   3   4   5
- Transparency: 0   1   2   3   4   5
- Qualifications: 0   1   2   3   4   5

YOU MIGHT BE A RED IF...

These phrases are effective with you:

- We've got a fantastic opportunity and challenge for you!
- This will allow you to really think outside the box!
- We know you'll do an excellent job!
- We believe you can spearhead this new opportunity!

These phrases really annoy you:

- Someone calls you lazy or unmotivated.
- You are referred to as boring, dull or uninteresting.
- Someone tells you their impression of you is that you seem scared or unsure of yourself.

FOOTNOTES

29. https://www.azquotes.com/quote/541654

MY NOTES

THE FOUR SAX VIRTUOSOS

Chapter 3

THE SECOND SAX VIRTUOSO

*I believe musicians have a duty,
a responsibility to reach out,
to share your love or pain with others.*
~ James Taylor[30]

- • -

AS BEVERLY OPENED THE FRONT DOOR of the music education establishment, she couldn't help but notice the yellow (it was actually Gold lacquered, but she saw it as yellow) saxophone on the wall. There was something about that saxo... It was as if a powerful improvised solo emanated from it and struck her, punching her deeply in her soul. She suddenly felt an overwhelming sense of *responsibility*. All the while, a soft jazz backing track played in the background. Beverly was momentarily mesmerized.

"Mom, what are you doing?"

The music suddenly stopped. Beverly shook her head and said,

THE FOUR SAX VIRTUOSOS

"Huh? What?" She saw Iggie's concerned look and managed to say, "Oh, it's nothing. C'mon, let's find out who runs this operation."

- • -

A short, stocky man was positioning a student's hands and wrists into the proper alignment on his saxophone when he made eye contact with his visitors. He raised his hand in acknowledgment of their presence, then gestured that he'd be right over.

The man was definitely in charge. All eyes were directed at him, at his every word. It's as if the students were spellbound – either that or they were hearing something for the very first time. They certainly listened intently and nodded repeatedly, seemingly after every pearl of wisdom the man shared with his disciples.

Beverly was impressed. She thought a student or two would tip over and fall from all the nodding and ensuing dizziness. All they needed was a small gust of wind. *Any moment now*, she thought. *Any moment now...* But no one fell.

The class size was about twenty students' strong, yet they looked like they were many more. They resembled a well-trained military band, with discipline and focus being the common denominators. The rows of chairs, as may be expected, were all straight as an arrow.

The man then raised a hand and an assistant stepped forward and was handed the baton. The man then walked away. The assistant assumed the band director's role and the class continued with the same format and procedures as before.

As the man approached his visitors, an ear-to-ear grin became apparent. Iggie couldn't help but notice a gold tooth - it glittered as the light hit it just right. The man said, "Hello. I'm Saxophone Virtuoso Yellow. How may I help you?"

Beverly stretched out her hand and they shook cordially. She said, "Hi. I'm Mrs. Beverly Song and this is my son, Iggie."

Iggie, hating the way his nickname sounded, interrupted her. "Ignatius, mother. Ignatius... not Iggie." He couldn't ignore the look of surprise in the sax educator's face, so he added, "Ignatius, sir. My name is Ignatius Song."

He offered his hand and the sax educator took it, giving him the warmest handshake he'd ever had. To Iggie, it was unexpectedly comforting.

SV Yellow
Ignatius. That's a good name.
A derivative of *ignited* – one
who is on fire! You like that?

Iggie
Yes sir.

SV Yellow
How old are you, fiery one?

Iggie
(*with a squeak in the voice*)
Twelve...
(*clearing his throat*)
... twelve, sir.

SV Yellow
Twelve! Not even a teenager yet.

Iggie
I'll be thirteen in four months!

SV Yellow
Children must respect
their elders, including
their mothers. Understand?

Iggie remained quiet, so his mother chimed in.

Beverly
Listen to the man, son!
He knows what he's talking about.

Iggie
Yes. Yes, sir.
I understand.

SV Yellow
Now that you're going to be
more respectful...
(*opens his arms wide*)
Welcome to
Yellow Saxophone Music Academy!

Beverly
Well, thank you!

SV Yellow
Please, follow me to my office.

Beverly and Iggie followed music educator Yellow into a clean and well-organized office. A plethora of awards, plaques, and certificates filled every nook and cranny.

SV Yellow
(*pulls a chair for Beverly*)
Please, be my guest.

As the music educator closed the door behind them, Beverly noticed the man's fedora – it was gray instead of the usual black she was accustomed to seeing musicians wear. It looked authoritative and full of wisdom, just like the man sporting it. It was also perfectly fitted atop the man's head.

The music educator looked good. His clothes were clean and neatly pressed. *Looking good is the first step in being a good musician*, she'd often say to Iggie. Although, *Looking fabulous is the first step in being a great musical prodigy!* is what she really wanted to say.

And although she had just met him, Saxophone Virtuoso Yellow had made a very favorable first impression. Beverly Song couldn't wait to get started with her list of questions.

- • -

Beverly
For starters, I'll have you know my
son is a musical prodigy, he's
won international competitions,
and
he's gonna perform
in Carnegie Hall one day!

SV Yellow
Hmmm... interesting.

Beverly
Why is that interesting?

SV Yellow
For several reasons.
First, musical prodigies have attained
a very high level of achievement
before adolescence.
(*turns to Iggie*)
Son, have you performed in public?

Iggie
(*hesitant*)
Yes...

SV Yellow
In what capacity?

Iggie
What do you mean?

SV Yellow
Were you the main performer?

Iggie
(*looks down*)
I was a rock once, then I was a tree.

SV Yellow
Any speaking or performance roles?

Beverly
Enough!
You've got to be kidding me!

SV Yellow
Mrs. Song, I don't kid about this.
Your son, as a 12-year-old, has probably
not demonstrated the special musical
talents you're attributing to him.

Beverly
At-tri-bu-ting?

SV Yellow
(*raises both hands defensively*)
And that's okay.
He can begin his musical
journey from this point on
and
we can see where that takes him.

Beverly
But... my son has spent
a lot of years doing this.

SV Yellow
I don't doubt it. But exceptional high levels
of musical achievement at an early age are
quite rare. These so-called *musical prodigies*
carry with them much responsibility
and (though it may sound counterintuitive)
a certain degree of *maturity*.

Beverly
My son *is*... mature!

SV Yellow
The disrespect he showed towards
you a while ago was not a sign
of maturity – it was a sign of *immaturity*.

Beverly
(*throws her hands up in the air*)
I can't believe this!

SV Yellow
Believe it. And there's more...

Beverly
What next?

SV Yellow
(*to Iggie*)
Ignatius, have you ever been a member
of a band or a musical ensemble?

Iggie
Yes, sir.

SV Yellow
What instrument do you play?

Iggie
Uhhh... it depends.

SV Yellow
It depends on what?

Iggie
On what I feel like picking up that day.
(*the cowbell flashed in his mind*)

SV Yellow
Oh, the *flavor of the month* approach?

Iggie
I'm sorry?

SV Yellow
Have you perfected one instrument?

Iggie
Ah... I dunno.

SV Yellow
(*to Beverly*)
Mrs. Song, at Yellow Saxophone Music Academy we recommend that students become highly adept at one instrument first - that would be the saxophone.
Then,
they can explore other instruments if they so desire.

Beverly
(*mumbles*)
I guess that makes sense...

SV Yellow
Okay, then...
(*back to Iggie*)

SV Yellow *(cont'd.)*
Ignatius, you've won an international music competition?

Iggie
Yessir.

SV Yellow
Where was this competition?

Iggie
Las Vegas.

SV Yellow
How many competitors in your division?

Iggie
One other kid. I think he was from Idaho or Utah. I don't know... but I beat him!

SV Yellow
Ignatius, do you believe you deserve to be called the winner of an international music competition when your competition was one other kid from the U.S.?

Beverly
(cuts in)
Wait a minute! The event was called a "World Music Championship" and he won! So, yes, he's a World Music Champion!

SV Yellow
Is that so?

Beverly
Yes! It's not his fault
no other countries showed up!
That's on the promoters.

SV Yellow
Mrs. Song, if your son enrolls at
Yellow Saxophone Music Academy,
he won't automatically be placed as 1st chair,
and he certainly won't be referred to as
a World Music Champion.

Beverly
Well... what would he start out as?

SV Yellow
Because here we strictly
follow tradition, he would start out
in the Beginner Saxophone Program,
and then we'll go from there.

Beverly
What?

SV Yellow
(*to Iggie*)
Son, have you ever played saxophone?

Iggie
No, but I know that you play
it with 3 fingers.

Beverly
(*frustrated*)
That's the trumpet, Iggie...
the trumpet!

SV Yellow
Very well, then.
The Beginner Saxophone
Program it is.

Beverly
But, why?

SV Yellow
All students need to develop
a solid foundation first, then they
can build on that.
It's why you don't build a house on sand.

Beverly
Who'd build on sand?

SV Yellow
Precisely! The rain, the floods,
the wind will come... and
the house will fall, right?
At Yellow Saxophone Music Academy,
we don't want any of our students falling.

Beverly
So, what makes up this
"foundation" you talk about?

SV Yellow
We first teach the proper way
to hold a saxophone and the proper
hand and wrist positioning. We help students
develop their *embouchure* - that's the manner
in which a musician applies the mouth
to the saxophone mouthpiece.

Beverly
I would imagine you just
put your lips together and blow...

SV Yellow
(*chuckles*)
There's a bit more to it than that.
You see, "embouchure" comes from the
French word *bouche*, which means "mouth."
It's really how we use our lips, facial
muscles, tongue and teeth on the
mouthpiece of the saxophone.

Beverly
Boy, there's a lot more
to it than what I thought.

SV Yellow
Yes. In fact, dental/oral hygiene
and anatomy of the oral cavity
also have a lot to do with
the sound produced by sax musicians.
We strive to help our students achieve
universally aesthetically pleasing sounds.

Beverly
Yes, aesthetics is good.

SV Yellow
Beyond aesthetics, we also teach students how to choose the right mouthpiece and the best reed for their particular needs - and how to maintain them and care for them. Plus, we ensure students develop proper body mechanics, balance, strength, alignment, focus, and coordination.

Beverly
Wow! That looks like you covered it all. I would guess that completes your definition of a "foundation?"

SV Yellow
Not quite. I still need to mention perhaps the most important thing: *Breathing.*
Proper breath control, breath support, and air flow are paramount to playing the saxophone at the highest musical level.

Beverly
Of course, breathing!
(*to Iggie*)
You breathe, don't you?

Iggie
Duh!

Beverly
(*punches her iPad aggressively*)
Very well... I still
have some questions.
May I?

SV Yellow
Sure. Go ahead.

Beverly
Why is your fedora gray?

SV Yellow
In the olden days, all beginner
sax players wore white fedoras.

Beverly
I did not know that.

SV Yellow
It turns out... the color white
represents purity and innocence.
The white fedora worn by beginners
represents knowledge waiting to be learned.

Beverly
So, they wear a white fedora so
knowledge will be absorbed by
osmosis into their head?
(*ponders aloud*)
Knowledge... waiting to be learned...
(*sudden outburst*)
I like it!

SV Yellow
Yes. Many music educators say
that the white fedora has no knowledge.
I like to say a white fedora is
knowledge *waiting* to be learned.

Beverly
Interesting...

SV Yellow
And when the student is ready,
(*looks at Iggie*)
the white fedora shall appear.

Beverly
That's a unique way
of looking at it.
Glass half full, eh?

SV Yellow
Right. Anyway, in the early days,
as the sax beginner students
practiced and gained experience and skills,
their fedoras began to... change.

Beverly
Change? How so?

SV Yellow
They got darker and darker.
The symbolism was that the originally
white fedoras were evolving. They were learning
and developing alongside the students who
wore them. In a way, those fedoras were

SV Yellow *(cont'd.)*
getting *stained* - stained with fundamentals,
scales, etudes, techniques, and long tones.
Lots and lots of long tones.
In a word, *knowledge*.
They were getting stained with knowledge.
In reality, the fedoras were
simply getting dirtier and dirtier.

Beverly
And it's not like you can just throw
a fedora into the wash! I suppose you can always
send it to be dry-cleaned...

SV Yellow
According to tradition, fedoras
should never be washed. If you
wash them, you'd be washing away
all the knowledge you gained.

Beverly
Really?

SV Yellow
Yes, and everything you had learned
in your musical journey would be lost forever.
All the good from the fedora, and all the
bad from the dirty clothes, would go
down the drain side by side.
You'd have to start all over again.

Beverly
Wow, I didn't know that.
(turns to Iggie)

Beverly *(cont'd.)*
Did *you* know that?

Iggie
Ahhh... no?

Beverly
(*turns to SV Yellow*)
So, as the fedoras got darker and darker, they eventually got to the darkest color... black.

SV Yellow
That's right.

Beverly
Wait a minute! If the fedoras get darker as you gain knowledge, and if black is the darkest color... why is your fedora gray?

SV Yellow
Because when you get to black fedora, contrary to what many people think, you're not done. You've only just begun. As a black fedora-wearing musician, your goal is to continue to learn and accumulate knowledge. If and when that happens, the black fedora will start to fade.
Eventually, it will look gray like this.
(*points to his fedora*)

Beverly
So, a gray fedora is a black fedora
with a lot of extra musical knowledge?

SV Yellow
Precisely!

Beverly
That's the first time
I hear of a gray fedora.

SV Yellow
Most music educators with many
years of training have noticed
their fedoras slowly turn gray.
In fact, I believe the gray fedora
is the missing link! It completes
the never-ending continuum of
learning, the circle from white to black,
from beginner musician to musical virtuoso.
(*turns to Iggie*)
Ignatius, do you like to paint?

Iggie
Yes, I take an art class at school!

SV Yellow
Very good! Do you get to mix
the assorted colors sometimes?

Iggie
Yes, I love mixing the colors
and making new ones!

SV Yellow
And do you know what you get
when you mix black and white
on your artist's color palette?

Iggie
Gray?

SV Yellow
Yes, gray.
Gray also means this –
(*takes off fedora and points to his head*)
gray hair.

Beverly
What does your hair
have to do with any of this?

SV Yellow
Gray also implies elderly...
and the elderly carry with them
a wealth of knowledge that
can only come with time.

Beverly
(*finds inspiration*)
Yes, time and
personal experience!

SV Yellow
You're getting it!

Iggie
So, a gray fedora is

Iggie *(cont'd.)*
old like your hair?

SV Yellow
(laughs)
Yes, that's it! But I'm not only
talking about the gray on top
of my head. I'm also talking about
inside my head, in my brain.
(turns to Beverly)
Mrs. Song, did you know
the part of the brain associated
with intellect is called the gray matter?

Beverly
Yes, I've... heard that. I think.

SV Yellow
This "gray fedora" phenomenon
is so innovative, so powerful!
And even though I'm a very
old-school saxophonist...

Beverly
(interrupts)
...old-school?

SV Yellow
You know, black hat and black glasses.
So, even though I'm a *traditional* sax man,
I also recognize when a change needs to be made.

Beverly
What change needs to be made?

SV Yellow
A change to the unwritten laws that
govern musicianship and achievements.

Beverly
Oh, you want to change
what's not written down!
(*facetiously*)
That makes sense...

SV Yellow
That is correct. I'm considering
putting it in writing and making
the gray fedora the official
symbol of musical mastery
in our
Yellow Saxophone Music Academy.

Iggie
Higher than a black fedora and sunglasses?

SV Yellow
Yes, the gray fedora will be
the highest honor. It makes perfect sense.
It's what's been missing since Day One.
Hopefully, other music educators and
saxophonists will see the merits of this
and adopt the gray fedora too.

Iggie
Wow, you're very smart!
(*turns to his mother*)
Smarter than my
old music teachers!

SV Yellow
Thank you. I figure that once our students achieve mastery of their instrument, they should also look the part... and a gray fedora is quite the fashion statement!

Iggie
(*to his mother*)
Mom, you always say...
(*mimics his mother*)
...looking good is the first step in being a good musician.

Beverly
Yes. Yes I do.
(*turns to her iPad*)
Very well then. Next question...
How good is this music academy?

SV Yellow
I don't understand your question.

Beverly
Well, is this academy nationally ranked?

SV Yellow
This is the best music academy in the entire state.

Beverly
(*taps some keys on her iPad*)
How so?

SV Yellow
Not only are our students
dedicated and trustworthy, they
always bring their A-game.
(*proudly*)
I'll have you know,
our students have won the
state championship
10 of the last 12 years.

Beverly
Impressive!

SV Yellow
I'm very proud of our students'
success, but I am not satisfied.

Beverly
Why not?

SV Yellow
The moment you're satisfied,
that's when you start your fall
from grace, when you start to
lose your winner's edge.

Beverly
Yes, that makes sense.
What kinds of competitions
does your academy participate in?

SV Yellow
Only solo and ensemble competitions

SV Yellow *(cont'd.)*
in accordance with the law.
The ones sanctioned by
National Governing Boards
of Music Educators.

Beverly
Sounds legit.

SV Yellow
Yes, ma'am, they are.

Beverly
Okay... next question:
What conservatory of music
did you attend?

SV Yellow
The New England Conservatory of Music,
in Boston.

Beverly
(*punches away at her iPad*)
Degree?

SV Yellow
DMA, Doctor of Musical Arts.

Beverly
(*tries to throw him off*)
Oh, not a PhD?

SV Yellow

My degree is more hands on,
performance oriented.
I played at a gig last night.
A PhD is for those who wish to go
into academia and do research.
That's not me.

Beverly

Moving right along...
Will my son be able to use the
instruments he already has?
I just bought him a very expensive
zither, direct lineage to the great
Johann Petzmayer, and I'd rather
not spend any more than I have to.

SV Yellow

If he already has a saxophone, he can
use that. No problem.

Beverly

He doesn't... have a saxophone.
(She thought, *But my Iggie has a damned cowbell!*)

SV Yellow

I'm sure we can work out
something with one of the many
excellent horns we have here.

Beverly

Alright...

SV Yellow
As you recall, Mrs. Song, at Yellow Saxophone Music Academy, we are very traditional. That means we help our students master the saxophone first. Once they've developed a solid foundation, they can learn other instruments. (SV Yellow thought, *Once you learn the saxophone, why would you want to do anything else?*)

Beverly
Roughly, how long would it take my Iggie to master that... that thingamajig?
(*waves her hand at nothing in general*)

SV Yellow
Every student learns the "saxophone" (*stresses the word*) at his/her own pace. However, we provide a detailed spreadsheet that helps our students log their progress.
(*opens a drawer, pulls out a paper, and hands it to Beverly*)
Here. Here's what I'm talking about.

Beverly
(*skims the spreadsheet; appears satisfied*)
Good...
(*continues her iPad notations*)

Beverly *(cont'd.)*
Last question:
Can you make sure there's no "heavy lifting"?
I don't want my son to get hurt.

SV Yellow
Mrs. Song, this is a music academy,
not a martial arts school.

Iggie laughed; Beverly didn't.

SV Yellow *(cont'd)*
While there may be some aches and pains
after prolonged practice of a musical instrument,
I assure you our teaching approach
prioritizes the prevention of *overuse injuries*.
Occasionally, someone may develop
CTS (carpal tunnel syndrome) or
a tendonitis, but we are careful and
we take preventive measures as much as we can.

Beverly
Yes, "preventive measures," but
can you *guarantee* me that my son
won't get hurt?

SV Yellow
Sorry to say, but in life
there are no guarantees.

Beverly
Well, can you at least promise me
you'll take care of his lips?

Beverly *(cont'd.)*
(grabs Iggie's lips and squeezes them)
Look at those plump, luscious lips.
Aren't they something?

SV Yellow
Yes, I believe we can help
prevent the various risks
to your son's lips.

Beverly
Very well, then. I guess we're done.
(gets her things and stands up)

SV Yellow
I appreciate your visit, and
I hope I've answered all your questions.

Beverly
Yes, yes you have.
We'll get back with you. Thank you.
(exits the office; Iggie follows)

SV Yellow
You're welcome.
We're here if you need us.

- • -

The PACE™ Palette gives the following attributes of *responsible* personalities, such as Saxophone Virtuoso Yellow. Here then, are the negative characteristics (the stressors, irritators, and aggravators) followed by the positive characteristics of Yellows:

Aggravators of YELLOWS

- Yellows get frustrated when others don't follow the rules.

- Yellows can't tolerate tardiness.

- Yellows expect you to be organized or you will lose credibility with them.

- Yellows often resist change.

- Yellows are typically perceived by others as "uptight" or too detail-oriented.

Strengths of YELLOWS

- Yellows value traditions, rules, and authority.

- Yellows are detail-oriented.

- Yellows are punctual and reliable.

- Yellows contribute to their community.

- Yellows provide stability within an organization or a school.

- Yellows are organized and methodical.

- Yellows implement guidelines and procedures in a systematic fashion.

THE FOUR SAX VIRTUOSOS

– • –

Here are a few questions to consider regarding the encounter between Beverly, Iggie, and Saxophone Virtuoso Yellow:

1) Do any of these positive or negative characteristics of yellow personalities sound like Saxophone Virtuoso Yellow?

2) What did Beverly Song like about Saxophone Virtuoso Yellow and/or his academy?

3) What did Beverly Song dislike about Saxophone Virtuoso Yellow and/or his academy?

4) Is Beverly Song likely to enroll Iggie in this academy? Why or why not?

5) Should Saxophone Virtuoso Yellow accept Iggie as a student? Why or why not?

6) On a scale of 0 – 5, with 0 being the absolute worst and 5 being the absolute best, how would you rate Saxophone Virtuoso Yellow in regard to the three markers of a good teacher mentioned in the *Introduction*?

- Respect: 0 1 2 3 4 5
- Transparency: 0 1 2 3 4 5
- Qualifications: 0 1 2 3 4 5

YOU MIGHT BE A YELLOW IF...

These phrases are effective with you:

- You can be in complete control and run with this one!

- We're confident you're gonna cross all your "t's" and dot all your "i's"!

- We need your help in holding everyone accountable for their role in this project!

These phrases really annoy you:

- Someone calls you irresponsible.

- You are referred to as uncaring or that you're not acting like a team player.

- Someone says you're inattentive or disinterested.

FOOTNOTES

30. https://quotefancy.com/quote/1440225/James-Taylor-I-believe-musicians-have-a-duty-a-responsibility-to-reach-out-to-share-your

MY NOTES

THE FOUR SAX VIRTUOSOS

Chapter 4

THE THIRD SAX VIRTUOSO

> *Nothing exists without music,*
> *for the Universe itself is said to have been*
> *framed by a kind of harmony of sounds,*
> *and the Heaven itself revolves*
> *under the tone of that harmony.*
> ~ Isidore of Seville[31]

- • -

AS BEVERLY OPENED THE FRONT DOOR of the music education establishment, she couldn't help but notice the blue saxophone on the wall. There was something about that saxo... It was as if a powerful improvised solo emanated from it and struck her, punching her deeply in her soul. She suddenly felt an overwhelming sense of *harmony*. All the while, a soft jazz backing track played in the background. Beverly was momentarily mesmerized.

"Mom, what are you doing?"

The music suddenly stopped. Beverly shook her head and said,

"Huh? What?" She saw Iggie's concerned look and managed to say, "Oh, it's nothing. C'mon, let's find out who runs this operation."

- • -

An obvious scuffle was taking place between two students. One was pulling at the other's neck strap while apparently attempting to retrieve something the other was holding in his clenched fist. It certainly didn't look like any musical learning environment Beverly had ever seen. A short, stocky man separated the students involved. He quickly managed to get them to stop their mutual aggressions. After giving them a brief lecture, he had them shake hands and then embrace in what looked like a reconciliatory hug. It seemed like things were back to normal, and the class of nearly twenty students resumed.

The man assigned an assistant to continue to supervise the students in question. He then walked towards Beverly and Iggie.

Beverly didn't notice the man coming in her direction. Her attention was entirely focused on the two students. She didn't like what she just witnessed and wondered if she should leave now. As she pondered her exit strategy, she heard, "I'm sorry you had to watch that. We've had problems with those two in the past."

Beverly turned toward the voice. It was the man who'd broken up the extra-curricular activities, the fight. She said, "What? Oh, I didn't see you come this way."

"Again, I apologize for what you saw. But hey, I am Saxophone

Virtuoso Blue. Welcome." He took Beverly's hand with both of his, giving her a welcoming two-hand greeting. She thought the handshake was quite authentic. He performed the same gesture with Iggie.

Beverly appreciated the music educator's handshake. She liked the fact that his entire attention was on the two of them at that moment – unlike people who shake your hand while looking the other way. Beverly never liked that.

SV Blue
And sorry for sneaking up on you.
You know, my students never see
me coming either.

Beverly
That's good to know… I guess.

SV Blue
Yes, being adaptable (like
a chameleon) is a good trait
to have. That's why I could
break up that fight before
it got out of hand.

Beverly
I see. Do you have
a lot of that…
(*waves a hand in the air*)
…going on here?

SV Blue
Sometimes. After all,
Blue Saxophone Music Academy

SV Blue *(cont'd.)*
is a place where students can
let out their frustrations.

Beverly
So, you encourage that?

SV Blue
Certainly not!

Beverly
Well then, what do you mean?

SV Blue
I love to help our students
solve their problems. First,
I encourage them to talk
about what's bothering them,
what's on their mind.
That's the most important thing.
Once we know that, we can help them.

Beverly
It sounds very much
like conflict resolution.

SV Blue
Yes! That's it!

Beverly
And what about when
they don't feel like talking?

SV Blue
That's when we encourage them
to let their music do the talking.

Beverly
How so?

SV Blue
By way of a musical challenge.
For example, the two students
you just saw...

Beverly
Yeah, how could we *not* see that?
(*turns to Iggie, who looks at the floor*)

SV Blue
They're our top 2 saxophonists.
And they're usually challenging
each other for the top spot
at this academy. One will be
1st chair for a month or two, then
the other wins the spot, and so on...

Beverly
So, that's what that
little tussle was about!

SV Blue
Well, this particular incident
had to do with our 2nd chair
needing a reed, so he "took"
one that belonged to our 1st chair
sax student - a rather expensive

SV Blue *(cont'd.)*
synthetic reed, mind you. But I
don't think he needed a reed.

Beverly
Why not?

SV Blue
Because the reed in question
is a size 3.5 and our 2nd chair
has never used anything
higher than a 3.0, even on
synthetics!

Beverly
So, what was that all about?

SV Blue
I believe it's a mental game.
Our 2nd chair doesn't really
need another reed - certainly
not a size he never plays.
Those two have a
chair challenge later today.

Beverly
I get it!
(*makes her notations*)
Do *you* challenge
other teachers too?

SV Blue
I personally don't like to compete.
To me, trophies and medals are not

SV Blue *(cont'd.)*
as important as helping my students
reach their goals.

Beverly
That's good to hear.
*(looks at Iggie; imagines
him shining bright on stage)*

SV Blue
Yes, at this point in my life,
it's about them, not about me.
(suddenly realizes something)
Sorry, I didn't get your name.

Beverly
Forgive me, I'm so rude.
My name is Beverly Song
and this is my son, Iggie.

Iggie, hating the way his nickname sounded, interrupted her. "Ignatius, mother. Ignatius... not Iggie." He couldn't ignore the look of surprise in the music educator's face, so he added, "Ignatius, sir. My name is Ignatius Song."

SV Blue
Well, nice to meet you both.
(turns to Iggie)
Ignatius, is there a particular
reason why you don't want
to be called Iggie?

Iggie
Gross – that's for losers!

Beverly
(*buds in*)
That's not for losers!

SV Blue
Mrs. Song, I'd like to hear him out.
(*puts hand on Iggie's shoulder*)
Ignatius, you really believe that?

Iggie
Yeah.

SV Blue
Yeah?

Iggie
I mean... yes, sir.

SV Blue
Why is that name a loser?

Iggie
I dunno.

SV Blue
Does it have to do
with other kids?

Iggie
I guess...

SV Blue
What do they say?

Iggie
(*mumbles*)
Iggie... Piggie.

Beverly
Iggie Piggie?
You're not fat!
Well, maybe a little... plump.

Iggie
You see, mother!

SV Blue
Alright, alright, I get it.
For now, you're Ignatius.

Beverly
I didn't know
they called you that.

Iggie
You never asked.

SV Blue
Perhaps it's better
if we go to my office.

Beverly
Yes, let's go.

SV Blue
(*cheers on a student before entering office*)
Good job, Roland!
That's what I'm talking about!

Beverly and Iggie looked back and saw the only tuba player giving a thumbs-up in their direction. *That was probably Roland*, Beverly thought, as they both followed SV Blue into his office.

The music educator's office was more "homey" than what Beverly expected. Several plants and flower arrangements added charm and created a welcoming ambiance. Of course, numerous certificates and plaques added the obligatory musical prowess credibility.

Beverly
There's no desk...
and no chairs!

SV Blue
That is correct.
I've found that I can
listen better if there's no
bulky desk between
my students and me.
Nothing gets in the way
of our conversation.
(*points to a throw rug*)
You can sit there.

Beverly and Iggie shrugged their shoulders in the "I dunno" gesture and proceeded to sit. Meanwhile, the music educator closed the door and grabbed another rug from a nearby closet.

He unrolled it and placed it next to the other rug, joining his guests on the floor. He sported a warm smile as he sat facing Beverly and Iggie.

- • -

SV Blue
It's mighty nice of you
to pay our academy a visit.
How may I be of service?

Beverly
Well, we're new in town
and we're looking for a music
school for my son here.

SV Blue
You've come to the right place!

Beverly
That's what we're trying
to figure out.

SV Blue
What are your goals, Ignatius?

Iggie
Ahhh... Carnegie Hall, for one.

SV Blue
Why Carnegie Hall?

Beverly
(buds in)
Because he's destined for
greatness! I'll have you know
my son is a musical prodigy and
he's won international competitions.

SV Blue
Wow!

Beverly
Yes. Impressive, right?

SV Blue
Yes, indeed!
(*to Iggie*)
How long have you been studying music?

Iggie
Most of my life.

SV Blue
Well, that sounds like a long time. How old are you?

Iggie
(*with a squeak in the voice*)
Twelve...
(*clears his throat*)
... twelve, sir.

SV Blue
Twelve!

Iggie
I'll be thirteen in four months!

SV Blue
(*to Beverly*)
At Blue Saxophone Music Academy,

SV Blue *(cont'd.)*
the youngest age to attain the top
position in a particular instrument
section is... 12-years-old.

Beverly
Twelve? Why?

SV Blue
It has to do with several
things – mainly loyalty.

Beverly
What does age have
to do with that?

SV Blue
Well, many music educators,
like myself, have been burned
in the past. Students nowadays
insist – heck, they demand –
the top spot, the 1st chair.

Beverly
If they deserve it,
what's wrong with that?

SV Blue
Nothing... if they remained
true to themselves and
to their teacher.

Beverly
I still don't get it.

SV Blue

It's complicated. The rank,
the chair, instead of going
into a student's heart or soul,
it goes to their head... and
not in a good way.

Beverly

Nonsense! My son
is a humble kid.
(*points to Iggie*)
Just look at him!

SV Blue

What happens is...
students reach the top spot,
the 1st chair, then they leave and
start teaching private lessons.
Many times, they compete
against their own music teacher!

Beverly

But this is America,
land of free enterprise.
A little competition
is good for everyone.

SV Blue

To me, life is not a competition.
It's about being better today
than you were yesterday.
As I said before, I don't like
to compete... and certainly
not against my own students.

Beverly
I can see that.
(*writes something on her iPad*)
Can we go over a
few more questions?

SV Blue
Sure, please do.

Beverly
Why aren't you wearing a fedora
or sunglasses?

SV Blue
(*laughs*)
And why am I not sporting
a soul patch or a goatee?

Iggie
What's that?

SV Blue
A *soul patch* is a few
whiskers just below the
lower lip...
(*points to his lower lip*)
...and a *goatee* is the soul patch
plus hair on the chin, like a goat!
Lots of saxophone players have them.

Beverly and Iggie
(*together*)
Why?

SV Blue
I guess to cover up the lower
lip irritation that can occur
from hours and hours of playing
the saxophone.

Beverly
(*points to her head*)
And the fedora?

SV Blue
Don't like hats. My head
gets really hot. And, I usually
wear shorts and a T-shirt. Tends
to make me less intimidating
to my students.

Beverly
I thought all musicians (music
teachers too) wore some sort of
instrument-specific attire.
A "uniform," if you will.

SV Blue
Most do. Not me.

Beverly
Alrighty then.
(*punches at her iPad*)
And... you have a
doctor's degree in music, correct?

SV Blue
No, I have a Masters degree.

Beverly
Oh, is that so?
(*aggressively jots something down*)

SV Blue
Yes, I chose not to go for
a doctorate. Too competitive.

Beverly
(*talks as she writes*)
Too... much... competition.
(*looks at SV Blue*)
Very well, then.
Since my son can't start out
at the top of the class, what
will his position, his ranking, be?

SV Blue
If he enrolls at Blue Saxophone
Music Academy, he will start out as
a beginner, like everyone else.

Beverly
Na-ah. I don't think so.

SV Blue
Yes, he'll be a beginner student
at our academy. But when he
participates in competitions, he'll
compete against everyone, including
the advanced music students.

Beverly
That's ludicrous!

SV Blue
It's ludicrous if he competes
against beginners when he's
studied music most of his life,
Mrs. Song!

Beverly
(*shocked*)
Oh?

SV Blue
Mrs. Song, at Blue Saxophone
Music Academy, your son will need
to demonstrate skill, learn our repertoire,
and our teaching approach first.

Beverly
And if I don't agree
with this crap?

SV Blue
Then I would be sorry
that you couldn't see
the value in what we do.

Beverly
(*writes on her iPad*)
Let's say I buy into this.
What then?

SV Blue
We have a unique system
here. We have a lot of city
champions! In fact, we're

SV Blue *(cont'd.)*
the best music school in the city!

Beverly
I was wondering
when you'd say that.

SV Blue
Excuse me?

Beverly
Your sign outside.
It says this is the best
music academy in the city.

SV Blue
The sign is right! We're definitely
not scraping the bottom of the barrel.

Beverly
How do you know you're the
best this city has to offer?

SV Blue
Because our students consistently
win the local competitions.

Beverly
Okay, got that.
(taps some keys on her iPad)
Next point: Will my son be able to
use the instruments he already has?
I just bought him a very expensive
zither, direct lineage to the great

Beverly (cont'd.)
Johann Petzmayer, and I'd rather not spend any more than I have to.

SV Blue
Yes, there's no need to spend more money on another instrument if he already has one... or several.
(*to Iggie*)
Do you have a saxophone at home?

Iggie
No...

Beverly
(*cuts in*)
No, he doesn't have a saxophone yet.
(*Where are all the good banjo teachers? she pondered.*)

SV Blue
Not to worry. We have an assortment of in-credible bluesy-sounding saxophones that we'd gladly let you try out.

Beverly
That's wonderful! Thanks.
(*makes notations on the iPad, then looks at SV Blue*)
With all the "informality" of this academy, I'm concerned my Iggie might get a little confused...

SV Blue
(*laughs*)
Con-fused! Of course not.

Beverly
Oh? How so?

SV Blue
Ignatius is young, and young students adapt well – better than adults.

Beverly
If you say so.

SV Blue
Sure! We're talking the stuff of legends here!

Beverly
(*speaks as she writes*)
Stuff... of... legends. Gotcha!
Okay, last question:
Can you make sure there's no "heavy lifting"?
I don't want my son to get hurt.

SV Blue
Mrs. Song, at Blue Saxophone Music Academy we're the opposite of cruel. We don't celebrate when students get hurt.
(*shakes his head*)
Here, that's a no-no.

Beverly
So, you're not cruel, but
can you *guarantee* me that
my son won't get hurt?
Because... that would be *cruel*,
wouldn't you say?

SV Blue
I wouldn't worry about
that. We have some of the
best ergonomic equipment
ever designed – and we
use it generously, too.

Beverly
For example?

SV Blue
Well, for one... we favor
neck harnesses over traditional neck
straps. While traditional neck straps
concentrate all their pressure
on the neck, the harness removes
undue pressure from the neck and
distributes it onto the shoulders.
Keeps pain-in-the-necks at bay.

Beverly
Certainly, a saxophone can't be
that heavy! Can it?

SV Blue
It depends on what saxophone
we're talking about.

SV Blue *(cont'd.)*
At Blue Saxophone Music Academy,
we start all beginner students
on the Alto Sax, which is
one of the smaller saxophones.

Beverly
Very well. So, it's on the smaller side.
(writes on her iPad)

SV Blue
Yes, but even small amounts of
weight dangling from the neck
for hours on end will start to
cause problems.
So, we avoid that
like the plague.

Beverly
Okay. Makes sense...
I guess we're done.
(gets her things and stands up)
We'll get back with you. Thank you.

SV Blue
(gets up, shakes Beverly's hand)
I hope you give your son a chance
to grow and explore his inner self.
Allow your son to embrace his
feelings, Mrs. Song,
like you embrace yours.

– • –

The PACE™ Palette gives the following attributes of *harmonious* personalities, such as Saxophone Virtuoso Blue. Here then, are the negative characteristics (the stressors, irritators, and aggravators) followed by the positive characteristics of Blues:

Aggravators of BLUES

- Blues do not like conflict.

- Blues are often sensitive to rejection.

- Blues don't like gossip.

- Blues don't like to compete.

- Blues don't tolerate cruelty to others or to animals.

- Blues don't like to be taken for granted.

THE FOUR SAX VIRTUOSOS

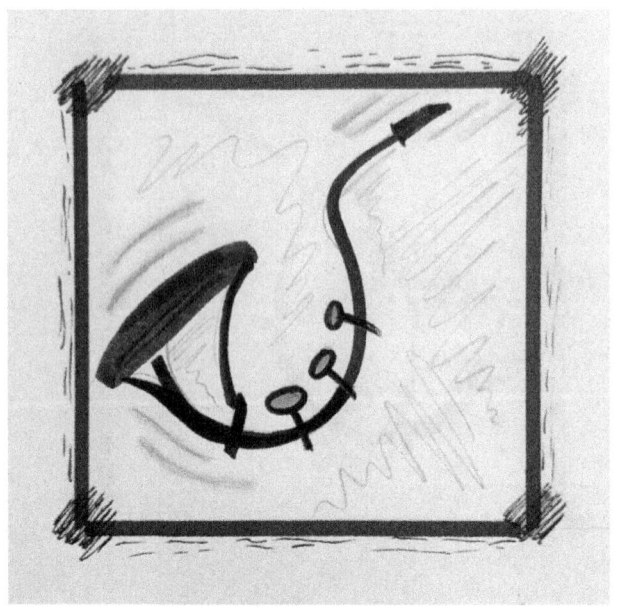

Strengths of BLUES

- Blues are very loyal friends; they value relationships.

- Blues embrace harmony.

- Blues are great mediators.

- Blues make intuitive and great listeners.

- Blues are great motivators of others.

- Blues are very perceptive.

- Blues have a great deal of integrity.

- Blues value loyalty.

Here are a few questions to consider regarding the encounter between Beverly, Iggie, and Saxophone Virtuoso Blue:

1) Do any of these positive or negative characteristics of blue personalities sound like Saxophone Virtuoso Blue?

2) What did Beverly Song like about Saxophone Virtuoso Blue and/or his academy?

3) What did Beverly Song dislike about Saxophone Virtuoso Blue and/or his academy?

4) Is Beverly Song likely to enroll Iggie in this academy? Why or why not?

5) Should Saxophone Virtuoso Blue accept Iggie as a student? Why or why not?

6) On a scale of 0 – 5, with 0 being the absolute worst and 5 being the absolute best, how would you rate Saxophone Virtuoso Blue in regard to the three markers of a good teacher mentioned in the *Introduction*?

   - Respect: 0 1 2 3 4 5
   - Transparency: 0 1 2 3 4 5
   - Qualifications: 0 1 2 3 4 5

YOU MIGHT BE A BLUE IF...

These phrases are effective with you:

- We need your input in resolving some people issues!
- What do you believe is fair in this scenario?
- We need you to really motivate the team in this project!

These phrases really annoy you:

- Someone calls you insensitive.
- You are referred to as inconsiderate or unsupportive.
- Someone tells you they feel you're rigid or unyielding.

FOOTNOTES

31. https://www.azquotes.com/quote/655071?ref=harmony-in-music

THE FOUR SAX VIRTUOSOS

Chapter 5

THE FOURTH SAX VIRTUOSO

> *These are the sort of things
> that push you on in music -
> the curiosity,
> a passion for new ideas.*
> ~ Elvis Costello[32]

- • -

AS BEVERLY OPENED THE FRONT DOOR of the music education establishment, she couldn't help but notice the green saxophone on the wall. There was something about that saxo... It was as if a powerful improvised solo emanated from it and struck her, punching her deeply in her soul. She suddenly felt an overwhelming sense of *curiosity*. All the while, a soft jazz backing track played in the background. Beverly was momentarily mesmerized.

"Mom, what are you doing?"

The music suddenly stopped. Beverly shook her head and said,

"Huh? What?" She saw Iggie's concerned look and managed to say, "Oh, it's nothing. C'mon, let's find out who runs this operation."

- • -

A short, stocky man opened the door to an office and let some people out. Beverly suddenly halted and Iggie ran into her, not expecting her to stop that quickly. The man had a walking cane in one hand and held the door open with the other. As soon as he bid farewell to his guests, he smiled at Beverly and Iggie, his new visitors. The overhead lights hit the man's face just right and Beverly couldn't help but notice the twinkle in the man's eyes as he said, "Hello. Perfect timing!"

The man walked effortlessly toward Beverly. All the while, she was thinking, *He doesn't need that cane. Who is he trying to fool? Heck, he walks better than me!*

The man said, "Saxophone Virtuoso Green, at your service." He enveloped Beverly's hand in both of his, the J-shaped cane swiftly dangled on his left forearm – Beverly never saw him put it there. He bowed deeply while shaking her hand. Beverly was flabbergasted. She had never felt so... important.

SV Green
Who do I have the
honor of meeting?

Beverly
Oh dear...
(*blushes*)
I am Mrs. Beverly Song
and this is my son, Iggie.

SV Green
Iggie... do you mind
if I call you Iggie?

Iggie
Ah... I prefer Ignatius.
That's my real name.

SV Green
Very well then, Ignatius...
(*takes his hand and bows
just like he did with Beverly*)
Welcome to
Green Saxophone Music Academy.

Beverly
No offense, but
you don't look like much.

SV Green
I'm sorry?

Beverly
I mean... you look like you
might be very ill...
with that cane and all.
Are you handicapped?

SV Green
(*smiles*)
Perfect!

Beverly
(*surprised*)

Beverly *(cont'd.)*
What? I don't think you
understand what I
just said about you!

SV Green
Oh, I understand.
I understand... perfectly!

Beverly
And why do you keep
smiling like that?

SV Green
Because I love not looking like much.
"Handicapped," as you put it.
I prefer to appear like a regular,
non-threatening person. That is
the perfect way I want to be seen.

Beverly
I don't get it.
You enjoy being put down?

SV Green
No, I don't think anyone does -
but I so enjoy catching others
asleep, off guard. It's called
the element of surprise.

Beverly
Yes, I've heard of that...

SV Green
Take this cane, for instance.
It looks like a simple walking
stick, a standard medical device.

Beverly
Well, it is!

Iggie
It keeps you from
falling on your face, right?

SV Green
Well, you're both right, but
it's also the perfect weapon!

Beverly
C'mon, a simple cane!
The perfect weapon?

SV Green
If it isn't, it's as
close as they come.

Beverly
You're serious!

SV Green
Show me any other weapon
you can legally take through
airport security.

Beverly
Ahhh...

SV Green
Can't think of any,
can you?

Iggie
How about... a saxophone?

SV Green
A saxophone... very good.
Very good.

Beverly
Wait, a saxophone is not a weapon!
(*looks at Iggie*)
Is it?

SV Green
I prefer not to use a saxophone
as a weapon, but in an emergency...
(*redirects the conversation*)
Coming back to the
airport security question.
Many saxophonists have a
difficult time boarding with
their instruments. I have found
that this cane not only takes
me straight to the front of the line,
but airport personnel are more likely to
allow my saxophone on board with me!
No questions asked.

Beverly
And *why* do you use
a cane? Are you

Beverly *(cont'd.)*
injured or something?

SV Green
Yes, I was shot in the leg.

Iggie
Wow! You've been shot at?

Beverly
What happened?

SV Green
A few years back, a crazy
person came into my church.
I was in the middle of my sax solo -
I play in church every Sunday.

Iggie
That is so cool!
I mean, playing in church... is cool.

SV Green
Yes, it is.
Anyway, my sax was awesome
that day! It was responding
differently.

Beverly
How so?

SV Green
It vibrated more than usual.
I believe it was an instrument

SV Green *(cont'd.)*
of the Lord at that precise moment.
It was playing - "singing" is a better
word - it was singing like
it never did before.

Beverly
(*anxious*)
So, what happened?
Out with it!

SV Green
Yes, I'm getting there.
This man came in with guns blazing,
shooting at everyone and at nobody
in particular. A few parishioners thought
they heard him say something about Allah.

Beverly
Oh my...!

Iggie
How did he shoot you?

SV Green
Well, he came right at the
Choir. Maybe he didn't like
what we were playing.

Iggie
That's not nice.

SV Green
At any rate, I had to do something.

SV Green *(cont'd.)*
So I took him down right away,
but not before he put
a bullet in my leg.

Beverly and Iggie
(simultaneously)
Wow!

SV Green
I went through a lot of
physical therapy and rehab.
That's when I met my
new friend.
(twirls the cane)
It's been my constant
companion ever since.

Iggie
*(amazed at the cane's
sudden action)*
That was cool!

Beverly
Okay, enough twirling.
(takes out her iPad)
Tell me...
(writes something on the iPad)

SV Green
(interrupts her)
Hold on.

SV Green suddenly begins to play a beautiful Alto Saxophone, which he seemingly retrieved out of nowhere in particular. Acoustically and aesthetically, it was the finest sax Beverly or Iggie had ever heard or seen. The sound was magical, and it inspired all the senses; and the engravings were sophisticated, yet simple. When SV Green finished playing, Beverly and Iggie came back from their roller coaster ride of emotions and sensations, and they were ecstatic! Iggie was nearly hyperventilating, and Beverly turned away to wipe a tear from her cheek.

Beverly and Iggie
(*together*)
Wow!

Beverly
(*in shock*)
I've never... experienced
something like that before!
What was it?

SV Green
(*smiles*)
I like to call it...
the element of surprise!

Beverly
Okay. I think I get it.
(*composes herself*)
When we first met, I have
to admit, I didn't think
you were much of...
anything, really!

SV Green
I kind'a figured that much.

Beverly
But after that music,
that sound... I gotta hand it
to you.
That was the most beautiful
thing I've ever experienced!

SV Green
Well, thank you!

Beverly
(looks up to the ceiling)
I was transported back
to grandma's house.
Oh, how I miss my dear grandma.

Iggie
(puts his hand on her shoulder)
Are you okay, mom?

Beverly
Yes. Yes, Iggie.
Thank you.
*(takes a deep breath,
then addresses SV Green)*
About your music school...
When we walked in,
I didn't see any students.

SV Green
Oh, they are there –

SV Green *(cont'd.)*
all 24 of them.

Beverly
All I saw was a bunch
of people standing around.
None of them are dressed
in musicians' attire.

SV Green
That's them. Class
starts in 5 minutes.

Beverly
But they're wearing
street clothes and shoes!

SV Green
Yes, they are.

Beverly
(continues)
And I see no musical instruments!

SV Green
No, you don't because today
our musical instrument
is our *voice*.
Once a week, all our students
receive voice training, regardless
of what instrument they're learning.

Beverly
Why?

SV Green
At Green Saxophone Music Academy,
we've found that when you can
hear what you actually wish
to sound like, you're more likely
to achieve your individual sax
sound much quicker.

Beverly
And how does your voice
help you hear what your
sax is supposed to sound like?

SV Green
Good question!
The saxophone is probably
the closest any musical instrument
can get to the human voice.

Iggie
Really?

SV Green
Yes, Ignatius...
and we have Mr. Adolphe Sax
to thank for that.

Beverly
Who is that?

SV Green
Only the inventor of
this great instrument!
(*looks at the clock on the wall*)

> ***SV Green** (cont'd.)*
> Class is about to start!

> ***Beverly and Iggie***
> *(at the same time,
> also look at the clock)*

> ***SV Green***
> I invite you both to
> stay and watch.
> The students are ready.

> ***Beverly***
> *(looks at Iggie; he nods)*
> Sure! We'd love to watch.

SV Green had one of his assistants bring chairs for the two guests. Surprisingly, Beverly hadn't felt this much anticipation since she was a little girl. She recalled her father's words, *Calm down, Bev. You don't wanna get electrocuted! Remember, anticipation is the electricity of children.*

SV Green clapped his hands twice, in staccato fashion, and all the students quickly formed a large circle around him. They stood at an alert and ready position, facing the center of the circle. None of them looked like the typical nerdy band kid. None of them needed to.

The music educator proceeded to lead warmups, which included strange sounds and facial expressions. They started out *yawning* and *sighing*, which activated Beverly and Iggie's autonomic nervous systems and led to them yawning and sighing along with everyone else.

This was followed by lip buzzing, humming, and tongue trills. But the funniest to Iggie was when everyone puffed out their cheeks and then opened up their mouths wide like a hippo. Iggie loved this class!

Beverly tapped at her iPad quickly. She was witnessing something not normally taught in everyday music classes. Beverly was floored. She wasn't quite ready for this approach of developing your own voice in order to find, then grow and develop your instrument's voice.

Beverly couldn't fathom how so much information, how such a treasure-trove of knowledge, could be offered at one location. Although fascinated, she realized that she still had to dot all her "i's" and cross all her "t's." Due diligence could not be ignored – not after she'd spent so many years on Iggie and on acquiring all his music accolades. So, after the class ended and the last of the students left the premises, she and Iggie met with SV Green once again.

- • -

The office was simple, but orderly. Except for a poster that read "Explore the Universe." and a statuette of a green saxophone in a corner, there was not much décor. All three sat around a table that sported three bottles of water, each atop a coaster, an arm's length from each person.

Beverly
I have a list of questions.
Shall we start?

SV Green
I'm ready if you are.
(*takes a sip of water*)

Beverly
Alright... For starters,
I'll have you know my
son is a musical prodigy and
he's won international competitions.

SV Green
Okay.

Beverly
Is that it? Aren't you
gonna say anything else?

SV Green
Okay, I'll say something else:
I thought you said you had
a list of questions.

Beverly
I do.

SV Green
Well, that wasn't a question.

Beverly
I realize that, but I wanted to
tell you some of his achievements.

SV Green
Why is that important?

Beverly
Because that way you'll know
right off the bat where he is in the

Beverly *(cont'd.)*
musical totem pole.

SV Green
Good point.
However, at Green Saxophone Music
Academy, there is no totem pole.
There are no ranks, no chair hierarchy,
no trophies, no nothing... only
musical skills and passion to be shared
with the world.
We teach our students to alleviate
other people's problems
through music.

Beverly
You're joking!

SV Green
Mrs. Song, music is therapeutic,
it makes the world go 'round.
It's no joke.
Our school is only for
serious students.

Beverly
My son *is* serious!
He's invested a lot of
years into this.

SV Green
I'm sure he is...
and I'm sure he has.

Beverly
And?

SV Green
And audiences don't care
how many trophies or
what accolades you have.
They just want to enjoy
the moment and forget about
their worries.

Beverly
(*throws her hands up in the air*)
I can't believe this!

SV Green
The fact of the matter is:
Stress is at an all-time high.
And music is a de-stressor.
If you fail to believe this,
then this school is not for you.

Beverly
Are you kicking us out?

SV Green
No. I'm telling you the
hard facts of the world
we live in today.
(*gets an idea*)
Here, let me show you something...

The music educator takes out a balloon from a desk drawer and blows it up until it is nice and big. He then ties a string to the end of the balloon and hands it to Iggie, who smiles like a kid who just received another participation trophy.

Beverly
What is this for?

Iggie
Mother, I can take it
with me and show it to...

And just before Iggie finished telling his mother how much he liked his new balloon...

POW!

Mother and son shook at the same time. They'd been startled by the sudden popping of the balloon. SV Green smiled as he showed them a straightened paper clip he'd pulled out of a desk drawer.

Beverly
What is the meaning of this?

SV Green
That's how fast everything can
change – in the blink of an eye.
One minute you're showing off
all your accomplishments, you're
swollen with pride like that balloon,
and the next minute you're being
shot at...with real bullets.

Beverly
You're exaggerating!

SV Green
(*points to his leg*)
Am I, really?

Beverly
Well...

SV Green
All the trophies, medals, awards,
certificates, you name it –
everything comes crumbling down
and they don't mean a thing
when you're looking up the
barrel of a gun.

Beverly
(*concedes*)
Okay... I guess you
made your point.
(*swipes at her iPad*)
Next point: Will my son be able to
use the instruments he already has?
I just bought him a very expensive
zither, direct lineage to the great
Johann Petzmayer, and I'd rather
not spend any more than I have to.

SV Green
We don't teach the zither here,
Mrs. Song. I'm sorry he won't
be able to use it at our academy.

Beverly
(*under her breath*)

Beverly *(cont'd.)*
What a waste!

SV Green
I'm sorry?

Beverly
Cut and paste!
(*lifts her iPad*)
I said "cut and paste."
I'm having trouble here...
(*pretends to struggle with the iPad*)

SV Green
Mrs. Song, even though he won't
be playing zither, your son will
be learning a lot of
practical and innovative stuff...
(*puffs out his cheeks*)
like voice-development exercises!

Beverly
(*exasperated*)
We'll see.
I'll put that on
the back burner.
(*turns to her iPad*)
Next question...
How good is this school?

SV Green
We're the best
at what we do.

Beverly
(*Thinks to herself, "Of course!"
but says...*)
Can you extrapolate?

SV Green
Okay, this is the best
music school on Main Street.

Beverly
(*taps some keys on her iPad*)
How do you know?

SV Green
Every year there is a music
festival downtown. All local music academies...
(*corrects himself*)
...all Main Street music academies
participate. And every year Green Saxophone
Music Academy gets
standing ovations and encore requests.

Beverly
That doesn't mean
your school is better.

SV Green
It does when none of the other
music schools get standing ovations
and encore requests!

Beverly
I see...

SV Green
They prepare their students
for competitions. I prepare
mine for the real world.

Beverly
Yes, I've heard you say
that a few times already.

SV Green
Right is right any way
you wanna look at it.

Beverly
Okay... I'll move on.
What kind of music degree
do you have?

SV Green
Unlike other music educators
on Main Street,
I don't have a Doctorate, and
I don't have a Master's degree.
I have a Bachelor's.

Beverly
Only a Bachelor's! Wow!
(*aggressively jots something down*)
School? What school?

SV Green
Brown.
Brown University in Providence,
Rhode Island.

SV Green *(cont'd.)*
It's a Bachelor's in Music Education.

Beverly
(talks as she writes)
Rhode... Island.
(looks at SV Green)
I'm not judging here, but...
Why only a Bachelor's degree?

SV Green
My Bachelor's degree from Brown is
comparable to higher degrees
from other universities.

Beverly
(incredulous)
Of course it is!

SV Green
Sure, let me explain.
As an Ivy League institution,
Brown is highly regarded.
My four years there were
very focused, very intense.
Plus, our student-to-faculty
ratio was the best in the Ivies.
On average, we had one teacher
for every 6 students.[33]

Beverly
Wow! Talk about
individualized attention!

SV Green
Yes! And one more thing
that a lot of folks don't realize...

Beverly
What is that?

SV Green
At Brown, all our undergraduate
teachers were Doctors in their
field - professors, if you will.
At other "respected" schools,
the undergraduate teachers
are actually graduate students!

Beverly
What!!!

SV Green
Well, let me re-phrase...
they were graduate students
when I went to school.
Nowadays, I don't know if those
institutions have updated their methods.

Beverly
I didn't realize that!

SV Green
Well, now you do.

Beverly
(*taps at iPad*)
Okay, last question:

Beverly (cont'd.)
Can you make sure there's no "heavy lifting"?
I don't want my son to get hurt.

SV Green
Mrs. Song, Green Saxophone Music Academy is a music school. We don't do heavy lifting.

Beverly
Good! So, you're *guaranteeing* that my son won't get hurt...

SV Green
No. I don't guarantee anything. What I'm saying is that we don't do the heavy lifting... but our fans often do!

Beverly
What do you mean?

SV Green
I mean... after a successful performance, our musicians will sometimes literally dive onto the crowd, only backwards. They love it!

Beverly
Oh, you mean, like a *trust fall*?

SV Green
Exactly like a trust fall!

Beverly
So that's what you meant
when you said the
audience did the heavy lifting!

SV Green
(laughs)
Yes! You got it!

Beverly smiled. She was proud of her mental acuity.

Iggie saw himself floating from person to person, atop his fans' outstretched arms. Arms that appeared to be reaching for the stars! In a way, they'd reached their star, Ignatius, the New Saxophone Extraordinaire! The fans loved Iggie! Iggie loved his fans!

SV Green
What I'm saying is:
Don't be surprised if your son,
Ignatius, becomes a fabulous
musician and performer one day...
and his fans absolutely
adore him!

Beverly
...and tossing him from person
to person would be one way
his fans would show their adoration?

SV Green
Precisely.

Beverly
I was afraid you'd say that.
Okay, I guess we're done.
(*gets her things and stands up*)

SV Green
Mrs. Song, at Green Saxophone Music
Academy, we strive to do the right thing.
I hope you choose what's best
for your son. Thanks for visiting us.

Beverly
You're very welcome.
And yes, I have a lot of
things to think about –
important decisions to make.
We'll get back with you...

Just as Beverly was going to bid farewell, she notices SV Green pick up the beautiful saxophone once again. He softly places the bell of the horn next to his ear. Eyes closed, he smiles as if intently listening. After a moment, he opens his eyes and Beverly takes her cue.

Beverly
I'm sorry. But what
was that all about?

SV Green
(*smiles*)
Oh, you mean what was

SV Green *(cont'd.)*
my Selmer Supreme Alto
Sax doing next to my ear?

Beverly
Yes... whatever.
(*waves her hands in the air*)

SV Green
This is my personal saxophone
and I have a special
relationship with it.

Beverly
Okay...?

SV Green
Let me ask you something...
Did you ever hold a seashell up to your ear?

Beverly
Of course! When I was a little girl.

Iggie
Me too!
Whenever we go to the beach.

SV Green
And what do you
hear when you do that?

Beverly
Well, according to my father,
we're supposed to hear...

Beverly and Iggie
(*together*)
...the quiet roar of waves
crashing on a distant beach.

SV Green
Yes! And just like that seashell
next to your ear, the bell of
my Supreme next to *my* ear
allows me to hear, not waves,
but beautiful, inspirational
saxophone sounds from
masters throughout history.

Beverly
Is that so?

SV Green
This Supreme,
(*raises it higher*)
is something special.
It's as if all the history
of the saxophone, all the
sounds it's ever created, is at
my disposal whenever
I want to listen.

Iggie
Wow!

SV Green
Yes, if you listen carefully,
you'll feel all the emotions

SV Green *(cont'd.)*
the virtuosos of the past
shared with the world.
All from simply putting
the bell next to your ear,
just like a seashell,
and believing.

Beverly
(utters as she writes)
You... must... believe.
(looks up at SV Green)
After what you played a
while ago, I'm a believer.
And now, I believe
we'll be on our way.
*(makes eye contact with
Iggie; they exit the office)*

SV Green
Good bye!
(yells after them)
Stay vigilant and always
continue to learn...
both of you!

- • -

The PACE™ Palette gives the following attributes of *curious* personalities, such as Saxophone Virtuoso Green. Here then, are the negative characteristics (the stressors, irritators, and aggravators) followed by the positive characteristics of Greens:

Aggravators of GREENS

- Greens do not like to appear incompetent or stupid.

- Greens often seem aloof or at arms-length emotionally.

- Greens don't like it when things are not positioned in a logical, sensible manner.

- Greens prefer less emotion during an interaction, and more facts or solutions.

Strengths of GREENS

- Greens are very curious and independent by nature.

- Greens love to solve problems.

- Greens tend to be reserved and have a calm exterior.

- Greens value intelligence and justice.

- Greens strive to do things the right way.

- Greens believe competence is indispensable.

- Greens are more rational and less emotional.

- Greens enjoy creating new and innovative ideas.

Here are a few questions to consider regarding the encounter between Beverly, Iggie, and Saxophone Virtuoso Green:

1) Do any of these positive or negative characteristics of green personalities sound like Saxophone Virtuoso Green?

2) What did Beverly Song like about Saxophone Virtuoso Green and/or his academy?

3) What did Beverly Song dislike about Saxophone Virtuoso Green and/or his academy?

4) Is Beverly Song likely to enroll Iggie in this academy? Why or why not?

5) Should Saxophone Virtuoso Green accept Iggie as a student? Why or why not?

6) On a scale of 0 – 5, with 0 being the absolute worst and 5 being the absolute best, how would you rate Saxophone Virtuoso Green in regard to the three markers of a good teacher mentioned in the *Introduction*?

- Respect: 0   1   2   3   4   5
- Transparency: 0   1   2   3   4   5
- Qualifications: 0   1   2   3   4   5

YOU MIGHT BE A GREEN IF...

These phrases are effective with you:

- We need your logical thinking!
- We'd like your help in solving a problem we're experiencing!
- Call us if you need us... otherwise, we'll leave you alone!

These phrases really annoy you:

- Someone calls you stupid or insinuates it.
- You are referred to as inept.
- Someone tells you you're overly dramatic or irrational.

FOOTNOTES

32. https://www.azquotes.com/quote/844381

33. https://admission.brown.edu/explore/brown-facts

MY NOTES

THE FOUR SAX VIRTUOSOS

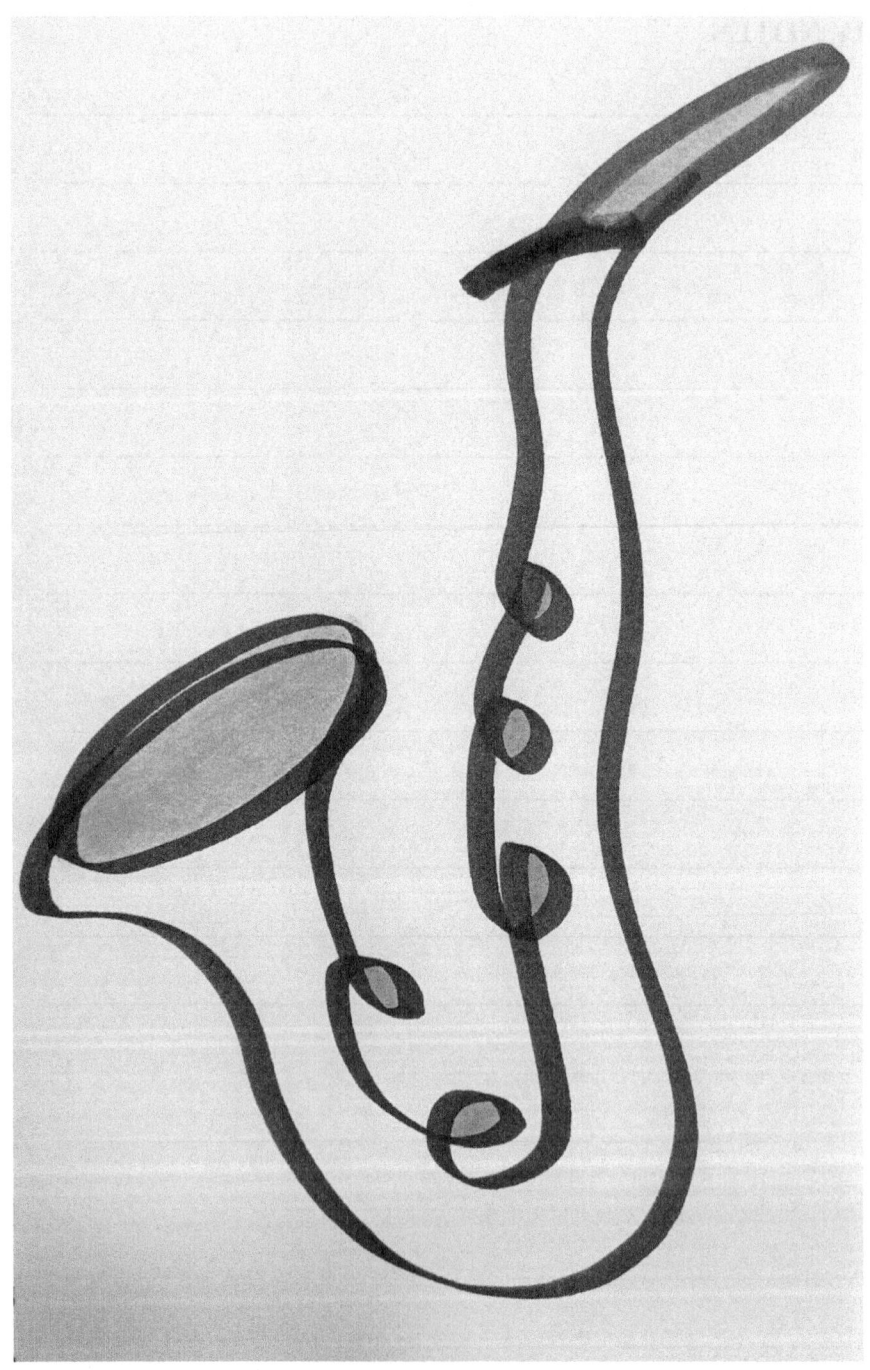

Epilogue –

Education is the most powerful weapon
which you can use to change the world.
~ Nelson Mandela[34]

- • -

THE MOTHER AND CHILD DEPICTED in *The Four Sax Virtuosos* are only one example of a typical scenario faced by music educators all over the world. By exploring that one scenario in four totally different points of view, based on the personality color of each of the four music educators, I hope you (the reader) gained new insight into how various music experts think, speak, and act. Believe me, I've personally experienced all four types, and combinations thereof.

You may have noticed that all four music educators had the same body habitus – that is, they were all short and stocky. This was only meant to nullify their physical attributes, so that neither one had a superior physical skill set over another. Essentially, in the physical sense, they zeroed each other out. And what we ended up with was four protagonists, each with classic traits of red, yellow, blue, and green personality types.

While *The Four Sax Virtuosos shares* some nuggets of musical wisdom, I challenge you to come up with additional situations and determine what solutions and/or ongoing problems you find from such encounters. For example, consider a father who is looking for a music program for his daughter, a recent bullying victim at her junior high school. (After all, young music students are often considered "band geeks" or "band nerds" by their peers... and they get bullied more than they should.) Thus, I encourage you to go through a possible scenario with each of the music educators and see where that takes you.

There are music educators who lead by example, and perform all the musical exercises, licks, and etudes alongside their students. Then there are those who literally sit in a chair – I've witnessed this – and spend the entire class period yelling out commands, instructions, and even throwing erasers at students (as was done with me) and causing them to quit band, never ever getting up from the chair!

So, I recommend that you review the characteristics of each personality type and then see which one applies to you. Music students should find out what color best defines their instructor. If you don't like what you have, change it. And because change is difficult for many people, you can start out with small, reachable steps. Gradual modifications will trump sudden changes any day.

My mentor, Jim Rohn used to say, "You cannot change your destination overnight, but you can change your direction overnight."[35]

I encourage you to adjust your direction, modify your techniques, improve your ergonomics and posture, optimize your breathing technique, learn new musical skills and etudes, practice long tones, and above all, always keep your reed wet - unless, of course, you have one of the new synthetic reeds that play instantly out of the box.

By changing with the times, you will constantly transform yourself into a better you, a better version today of yesterday's reflection on the mirror... and that can only happen when you continually challenge your mind, body, and spirit.

FOOTNOTES

34. https://www.brainyquote.com/quotes/quotes/n/nelsonmand157855.html
35. https://www.brainyquote.com/authors/jim_rohn?img=null

MY NOTES

SAXOPHONISTS SPEAK –

Music expresses that which cannot be said and on which it is impossible to be silent.
~ Victor Hugo[36]

- • -

SAXOPHONE VIRTUOSOS AND MUSIC EDUCATORS teach similar strategies to novice musicians, especially if the students are serious about their music education. Here are some of the recommendations from the experts:

- Maintain optimum health – for obvious reasons. Musicians with lung disease/infection may not be able to play their wind instrument during an acute exacerbation.
- Engage in proper body mechanics and posture. This can prevent overuse syndromes and chronic painful conditions.
- For immediate feedback during practice, use a mirror. Videotaping yourself can also reveal bad habits you may not have been aware of. Thus, you can correct your deficiencies and your subsequent practices/performances will be that much better.

- Keep your instrument(s) in good working condition – this includes taking your instruments(s) for maintenance checks on a regular basis.
- Learn your scales in all keys. Why? Because scales make up the *foundation* of all the music we love to listen to and play in Western cultures.
- Practice regularly, even if only for 15-30 minutes per day. Daily short-duration practices are better than one long session once a week.
- Always keep your cane reeds wet. Synthetic reeds apparently don't require such moisture conditioning.
- For wind instruments, avoid eating while playing or performing. If you must eat, brush your teeth before returning to your instrument. Once, prior to playing saxophone at a wedding in outdoors Las Vegas (in 100+ degrees), the groom saw me brushing my teeth in the restroom. Besides experiencing pre-wedding jitters, he asked why I was doing this so soon before his nuptials. I mentioned I had just eaten a snack and I was brushing my teeth and cleaning my mouth in order to prevent food particles from entering my saxophone and interfering with the sound and the lifespan of the pads.
- Practice long tones in order to achieve consistency with pitch, color and body of your sound. Also, make sure you practice long tones with balanced reeds. Balanced reeds will optimize the interaction between your embouchure pressure and air pressure, stabilizing the two.

- For wind instruments, develop proper breath control. Inhale by using your diaphragm (i.e., don't lift your shoulders when inhaling – that implies you're breathing with your chest). Then, control the rate and pressure of your exhalation.
- Listen to lots of music – especially listen to musicians who play the same instrument you play. Yes, imitation is the highest form of flattery. First imitate, then create.
- To play fast, go slow. That is, in order to develop speed and dexterity in your fingers, you must practice playing it slowly at first. Many experts say: If you can't do it slow, you can't do it fast.
- Establish the melody first, then you can change it. This is especially true when you want to put your stamp (i.e., express your own *style* or *personality*) on a well-known song. And remember, don't change the melody too much since you'll risk playing something that doesn't resonate with your audience and/or is completely unrecognizable.
- Always clean your instrument thoroughly after each practice or performance. This is especially true for wind instruments.

- • -

Besides the above-mentioned recommendations, I believe saxophonists need to engage with other saxophonists and exchange ideas and strategies. *We must network to make the dream work.*

THE FOUR SAX VIRTUOSOS

Since I practice Medicine in rural America, it is not easy to find networking opportunities with other musicians in town. So, one way I network with musicians is in social media. I am a member of several worldwide saxophonist groups, and the other day a group member posted a query that sparked my interest.

Here it is: *Why do you play music?* My response was, "Because everyone deserves a chance to live to the fullest every once in a while."

Additionally, here are a few other noteworthy comments (in response to this post) that I wanted to share with you:

1. When I was 13, my father committed suicide. Up until that time I dreamed of being a professional athlete, but after his death I could no longer perform, due to intense physical pain. A voice inside me said, "Play music." So, I took up the saxophone. It saved my life and 50 years later, it's still with me. ~D.C.

2. I became epileptic at 16. The seizures became too much for me and I was constantly on medications which, if I missed a dose, I'd get seizures which wiped out my memory. I got a really bad one at 18, after which I couldn't even recognize my own sister for about an hour. I really felt like a slave... I spoke against it in the name of Jesus like a mad man speaking to himself, then I threw away my medications. Music was the only thing that gave me peace. I gave up everything, picked up the saxophone I had been gifted, and walked away from it all. I started a new life – just me and my sax. Fourteen years later, I've never had a seizure, totally healed. Wife and 2 kids who I provide for by

solely playing sax. It's more than a job to me, more than a hobby. It was my way out, the path to walk away from it all. And I still play my sax today. ~ D.W.O.

3. *My grandfather was a sax player and pianist. He passed away a few months before I was born. Grandmother always said I had all his mannerisms. And grandfather would play sax all day long each and every day. So, she gave me his sax. When I blew into it for the very first time, I was 10 years old, I felt the universe warp and I was transported to a familiar plane of existence. It was like returning home after a lifetime of being away. I am the reincarnation of my Grandfather. ~A.C.*

4. *My first solace. The only thing I had to look forward to over many years. It saved my life several times. ~J.K.*

5. *Because with music I experience my spiritual self consciously. Some would call it heaven on earth. I've had out-of-body experiences during gigs. ~A.L.*

6. *It's been my mental therapy since high school. I've learned everything I need to know in life from playing and practicing music. ~S.N.*

7. *Good question! Why do you breathe? ~M.K.*

- • -

THE FOUR SAX VIRTUOSOS

Each one of us has our own life, our own experiences, our own story. It is up to us what we do with our story. Do we want to tell our story to others? If so, why?

Do we want to share our story in the hope that perhaps we can help others? If we can do it, then certainly somebody else can do it, right? All it takes is one person to open the door, then others can walk through.

Before 1954, nobody believed any human could run one mile in under 4 minutes. It was humanly impossible. Nobody had ever done it! Then, Roger Bannister[37] broke that barrier in 1954 and suddenly the world realized the impossible was now possible. And now, many runners have successfully run a mile in under 4 minutes. Why? Because they *know* it's possible. The door has been opened!

Why do you want to play music? As you've seen in these pages (especially in the *Introduction*), there are many health benefits to playing music, not only to the musician but also to the audience. And at the end of the day, every person must decide what direction their life will take. Will that road include music? If so, make sure it's what you want and not what somebody else wants. In *The Four Sax Virtuosos*, Beverly Song wanted music for Iggie much more than Iggie wanted it for himself.

On the other hand, if music is something for you, then it is my desire that *The Four Sax Virtuosos* can give you some guidance and inspiration in your musical journey. In fact, the door is open. Now, study your craft and practice with discipline... and walk through the door.

Rock on!

FOOTNOTES

36. https://www.brainyquote.com/quotes/victor_hugo_106867

37. https://www.history.com/this-day-in-history/first-four-minute-mile

José Luis Hinojosa, MD, MHA
Physician Leader, Martial Arts World Champion
Keynote and Motivational Speaker
Musician, Author and Illustrator

ABOUT THE AUTHOR –

Don't forget – no one else sees the world the way you do, so no one else can tell the stories that you have to tell.
~ Charles de Lint[38]

- • -

JOSÉ LUIS HINOJOSA, MD, MHA and his family emigrated from Mexico to the USA when he was only 7 years old. He was fortunate to attend an Ivy League school (Brown University) for his undergraduate studies, after which he matriculated at the University of Cincinnati College of Medicine (Cincinnati, OH) to earn his Doctor of Medicine degree. After completing his Family Medicine specialty in McAllen, Texas at the South Texas Family Practice Residency – University of Texas Health Science Center, an affiliate with UTHSC in San Antonio, Dr. Hinojosa had a successful private practice for 25 years in south Texas. His clinic was named Hollywood Medical Center... where every patient is a star!

After almost 1,000 deliveries as part of the Obstetric component to his practice, Dr. Hinojosa retired from delivering babies after more than 17 years of doing it solo. He also achieved many medical accolades, with some of his defining moments in medicine being:

- 1993-1998. Doctor Hinojosa was a world-renowned Sports Medicine physician and traveled all over the globe as the Official Doctor for the United States National Tae Kwon Do Team (the same team that represents our country in the Olympic Games). He cared for our elite athletes during three World Championships and a World Cup.
- 2009. Doctor Hinojosa was named one of *America's Top Family Doctors* by Consumers' Research Council of America in Washington, DC.
- 1985-present. Doctor Hinojosa has been ringside physician for professional boxing and for MMA (mixed martial arts) "cage fights." Because of his martial arts background, he is highly sought out for these events.

In 2013, Dr. Hinojosa and his wife, Maria Elena, moved to Kansas, where he was Chief of Staff at the hospital and Medical Director at the clinic. He continues to practice medicine to this day. A firm believer in lifelong learning, Dr. Hinojosa attained his Master of Science in Healthcare Administration degree from Grand Canyon University in April 2016. He graduated with a 4.0 GPA.

Besides being a physician leader, Dr. Hinojosa is also a musician - he plays Alto Saxophone, Tenor Saxophone, and Clarinet. He joined band in junior high school because his parents did not allow him to try out for the football team, which was the direction his friends were taking. Since his older brother was already 1st chair Trumpet, Dr. Hinojosa opted to do something other than trumpet. So, after seeing how much fun Benny Goodman was having Saturday mornings on the TV set, Dr. Hinojosa chose the clarinet as his instrument. Unbeknownst to him, boys were not supposed to play clarinet those days and, in that city, - not then, anyway. On the first day of school, Dr. Hinojosa found himself as the only boy... surrounded by 25 girl clarinetists! He also achieved and maintained the coveted 1st chair Clarinet spot for years. However, a lot of the male classmates (who were not in band) began to bully him, eventually backing off when Dr. Hinojosa finally retorted, "You're just mad because I'm surrounded by all the pretty girls... and you're not!"

Soon thereafter, a local band was looking to expand and add a brass section. They'd asked around and learned that Dr. Hinojosa's brother was the best trumpet player around, so they recruited him. When they learned their new trumpeter had a younger brother (who, for all practical purposes, was considered a twin brother), they asked if Dr. Hinojosa played an instrument. "Clarinet... 1st chair," he proudly announced. The two band representatives silently looked at each other, then simultaneously said, "Nahhhh." Then they added, "But, if you can get a hold of a saxophone, we'll give you a chance." So, that's how Dr. Hinojosa picked up the saxophone and joined a professional band at the age of 14.

Dr. Hinojosa played professionally in weddings, quinceañeras, and many other celebrations throughout his high school years, but stopped his musical journey once college started. He believed music would take away valuable time from his goal of becoming a family doctor. And then, as is usually the case, life happens... and 42 years went by without the joy or benefits of playing music. Dr. Hinojosa picked up the saxophone once again after all those years and he is loving every minute of it. He kicks himself for having put aside one of his loves for so long. We all make mistakes in life.

Dr. Hinojosa is also a martial arts leader. He has trained and taught the martial arts for more than 40 years (yes, the time he spent away from music was the time he spent in martial arts) and has won many titles throughout five decades of competition. Some of his most notable wins comprise *World Championships* in Germany and México, multiple Hall of Fame awards, including a *Lifetime Achievement Award*, and he is a crowd favorite with his powerful, creative, and highly entertaining routines – most notably, his award-winning form entitled *Reflections of an Old Man*, where he dresses up as an elderly man with a cane and dazzles the crowd while reminiscing about his youth. Speaking of youth, Dr. Hinojosa has three children (JL, Laura, and Alexis) who always inspire him; he is also happily married to Maria Elena Hinojosa.

As an innovator, Dr. Hinojosa invented the popular game *Grand Champion®*, the first ever card game related to the martial arts. His motivational book, *Master and Disciple*, like *Grand Champion®*, teaches good moral values and became so highly acclaimed that in 2008 Dr. Hinojosa was inducted into the Universal Martial Arts Hall of Fame as *Author of the Year* because of the teachings and lessons found in *Master and Disciple*.

This book, *The Four Sax Virtuosos*, marks the 17th book authored by Dr. Hinojosa. He is a playwright: *Rosi Milagros* – a two-act play that takes place in 1924 México; and *Exam Room 2* – a one-act play about an elderly couple who find themselves lost in the healthcare maze. He co-wrote the screenplay for an independent feature length film (*Campeón: A Journey of the Heart*). He has also penned three books entirely (yes, 100%) in Spanish – they are *La Cabrona Virus* (this book is part fiction, part non-fiction, and part comedy; it's about a medical condition you didn't know existed), *¡El*

Lenguaje de losTriunfadores! (the Spanish version of his highly-popular personal improvement book, *The Language of Winners!*) and *Maestro y Discípulo* (the Spanish version of *Master and Disciple*).

In 2017, Dr. Hinojosa wrote *Physicians' Guide to Avoiding Lawsuits*, an easy-to-read roadmap for healthcare professionals that teaches eight simple secrets to avoid the courtroom! His tell-all memoir, *Fighting to Heal: The Story of Dr. Pepe*, was also published in 2017. For more information on how to get ahold of any of Dr. Hinojosa's books, please go to **www.BooksByDrHinojosa.com**

Dr. Hinojosa is a stage actor and has also appeared in several feature-length films. His most recent acting work was in the world premiere run (Nov. 2011 and Jan. 2012 in three south Texas cities) of *Tales of the Hidalgo Pump House*, where he played one of the lead characters, Luis Rivera, and had the opportunity to display his singing, dancing, and comedic timing. In his most recent film, he played the villain in the feature-length 2009 Warrior Pictures film *Campeón: A Journey of the Heart*.

As a professional speaker, Dr. Hinojosa is equally fluent in Spanish as he is in English keynote presentations. He shares his experiences with his audiences with such passion and clarity, that he always "connects." It is no wonder that Dr. José Luis Hinojosa is highly sought out as a motivational and inspirational speaker not only in the USA, but also in México. He is a specialist in *Leadership and Success* topics, with his most popular keynotes being: *The Making of a Leader, Dream Your Way to Success, The Five Business Lessons to Learn from Breaking Boards,* and *Develop a World Champion Attitude*. Likewise, with the release of *Physicians' Guide to*

Avoiding Lawsuits, Dr. Hinojosa looks forward to giving presentations to his colleagues on minimizing their risks of being named in a lawsuit. Please contact Dr. Hinojosa at his website, under the "Contact Us" tab:

www.BooksByDrHinojosa.com

FOOTNOTES

38. https://www.azquotes.com/quote/176752

THE FOUR SAX VIRTUOSOS

Musical Wisdom from the Experts

- • -

Dear Reader, was this book helpful to you?

- Friends and music colleagues, are you inspired to find out what your personality color says about you?

- Did this book help you understand the importance of doing your due diligence when choosing a music school or a music teacher?

- Would you recommend this book to your family, friends, and colleagues?

For volume discounts, to hire Dr. Hinojosa as a speaker or musician, or for any other questions, please contact him at:

www.BooksByDrHinojosa.com

At the website, please click on the "Contact Us" tab and send your e-mail today... and *congratulations* on taking this major step towards your personal growth and development. Thanks!

Also by José Luis Hinojosa, MD, MHA

NOVELS

The Tonic

PLAYS

Rosi Milagros
Exam Room 2

NONFICTION

The Four Grandmasters
Physicians' Guide to Avoiding Lawsuits
Fighting to Heal: The Story of Dr. Pepe
The Language of Winners!
¡El Lenguaje de losTriunfadores!
Report Card on Rape
Magnets for Health
Tae Kwon Do for Everyone
Frozen in Time
The HELP Secret

FICTION

La Cabrona Virus
Master and Disciple
Maestro y Discípulo

Picture of the Group Leaders mentioned
in the *Prologue*.
The leis around our necks represented
the four personality colors.
The wine bottles were our "participation trophies."

One of the promotional photos for the very popular group, *Chicano Breed Band*, from south Texas in the early 1970s. I am second from the left - yes, the one with the white belt and the flute. At that time, I played Alto Sax, clarinet and flute.

Made in the USA
Coppell, TX
06 October 2021